Rainbow Essence

Rainbow Essence

The Life and Teachings of Jatsön Nyingpo

Translated by Lama Yeshe Gyamtso

KTD Publications, Woodstock, New York

Published by: KTD Publications
335 Meads Mountain Road
Woodstock, NY 12498, USA
www.KTDPublications.org

Front cover image, page iii image: Jatsön Nyingpo
Back cover: HUM by Sange Wangchuk

ISBN 978-1-934608-53-1
Library of Congress Control Number: 2017963952

Printed in the USA on acid-free, 100% PCR,
FSC Recycled Certified paper

Contents

Translator's Introduction

The title *vidyadhara,* "bearer of awareness," is accorded only the greatest of vajrayana masters. The vidyadhara Jatsön Nyingpo was one of the greatest tertöns of the seventeenth century. A tertön is a revealer of terma: concealed teachings and other sacred objects. Jatsön Nyingpo's revelations continue to be widely practiced throughout the Himalayan region, and even in other parts of the world.

His teachings spread throughout many branches of the Nyingma, Kagyu, and other Tibetan Buddhist schools, and formed part of the spiritual practice of many great teachers, including Jamgön Lodrö Taye and the Fifteenth Karmapa Kakhyap Dorje.

His collected revelations are usually referred to as the Six Volumes of Jatsön Nyingpo. These include the *Very Profound Embodiment of the Three Jewels*; the *Peaceful and Wrathful Deities: The Essence of the True Meaning*; *Mahakarunika: The Self-Liberation of Lower States*; *Amitayus: A Vajra of Meteoric Iron That Brings All Siddhis*; *Hayagriva, Vajravarahi, and the Wish-Fulfilling Jewel*; and the *Glorious Intersex Protector*. Each of these six cycles has many parts; included with them are his other revelations, such as *Gampopa's Secret Path of Gurusadhana*, the *Eight Dispensations: The Essence of Siddhi*, and the *Black Hum Heart Essence*.

In addition to his revelations, Jatsön Nyingpo wrote commentaries, essays on Tibetan religious history, and a number of memoirs. These include accounts of some of his previous lives, his recollections of being with his teachers, and what he classified as his fourfold memoirs.

As readers will discover, he called his actual autobiography his Outer Memoir. It is translated in its entirety in this book. Readers will also discover that he finished it and then added more to it several times; I have called these sections Chapter One, Chapter Two, and so on, and indicated the years they deal with. His last entry was while he was in his fifty-seventh year, in 1642 C.E.

Jatsön Nyingpo called his collected songs and written advice his Inner Memoir. This is not translated here, but many examples of his songs are to be found in these pages as they are also part of the autobiography itself.

His Secret Memoir is an account of some of his visions and visionary dreams. I have translated part of this: his account of a dream he had upon completing his intensive practice of the *Embodiment of the Three Jewels*.

His Very Secret Memoirs are twofold: one is an account of a prophecy he received concerning his monastery in Kongpo in southern Tibet, Bangri Tashi Öbar; the other is an account of how he revealed terma. I have not translated either of these here as Jatsön Nyingpo made it extremely clear that they were not intended for public dissemination. However, I have included an account of the discovery of the *Embodiment of the Three Jewels* written by

Dakpo Norbu Gyenpa, the rebirth of the renowned Dakpo Tashi Namgyal. Norbu Gyenpa was one of Jatsön Nyingpo's main gurus, and also became one of his principal dharma heirs. This account agrees in every respect with Jatsön's own.

There is no cause to doubt the year of Jatsön Nyingpo's birth, 1585 C.E., but there are discrepancies among even the best sources regarding two equally significant dates: the year of his discovery of the *Embodiment of the Three Jewels*, the first of his revelations and even now the most commonly practiced; and the year of his death.

Jamgön Lodrö Taye, in his *Lives of the Hundred Tertöns*, gives the year 1620 C.E. as the year of this revelation. However, several editions of Norbu Gyenpa's account, written during Jatsön Nyingpo's life, date it twelve years earlier: 1608. Both were Monkey Years, and Jatsön Nyingpo states clearly in his *Very Secret Account of My Revelations* that this revelation occurred during a Monkey Year; he just doesn't say which one – 1608 was an Earth Monkey Year; 1620 a Metal Monkey Year.

In a colophon to his terma the *Essence of the True Meaning*, which was discovered at the same time and place as the *Embodiment* (but not disseminated until much later), the tertön gives the year of its discovery as the Earth Monkey Year. Nevertheless, as His Holiness the Seventeenth Karmapa Ogyen Trinley Dorje remarked to me a few years ago, 1608 sounds too early and 1620 too late.

What His Holiness was referring to is the fact that by his own account Jatsön's many years of solitary retreat only began in 1608, his twenty-fifth year. On the other hand, we know based on Norbu Gyenpa's account that he taught the *Embodiment* at

Daklha Gampo, Gampopa's seat, in or before 1623. Since we also know that, by Jatsön's account, he practiced the *Embodiment* secretly for years before teaching it, and since specific omens were required before he could disseminate it, a mere three years between discovery and dissemination sounds too short.

Here, in translating Norbu Gyenpa's account, I will use the date 1608, since three out of the five editions of it that I have consulted give that date: the Earth Monkey Year, as opposed to the Metal Monkey Year.

In his *Lives of the Hundred Tertöns* Jamgön Lodrö Taye gives the year of Jatsön's death as the Fire Monkey Year, 1656, his seventy-second year. Numerous other Tibetan and English language sources written since and drawn from Lodrö Taye's account have given the same date. However, in his account of Jatsön's final days, which I have translated here, Tsele Natsok Rangdröl (whom we believe to have been a previous life of Jamgön Lodrö Taye), who knew Jatsön well and was one of his most eminent disciples, clearly gives the year of Jatsön's death as 1646, his sixty-second year. Therefore, in translating Tsele's account, I have translated his statement that Jatsön Nyingpo died in the Fire Dog Year, 1646, without alteration.

The seventeenth century was a time of turbulence in Tibet. In particular, Tibet became swept up in the wars between opposing factions among the many Mongolian tribes because of the allegiance of various Mongolian leaders and tribes to different traditions of Tibetan Buddhism. Of principal importance to Jatsön Nyingpo's account of his later life is the conflict between Gushri Khan, the leader of the Koshuts, and Choghtu Khong Tayiji, a

Khalkha prince. In 1637 Gushri Khan successfully invaded and conquered Amdo, in present-day Qinghai, and defeated and killed Choghtu. Subsequently, in 1642, Gushri Khan invaded central Tibet and defeated the powerful king of Tsang, allowing the unification of Tibet under the theocratic government that continued to rule that country until the disastrous events of the mid-twentieth century. To understand Jatsön Nyingpo's reaction to this conflict it is helpful to remember that Choghtu Khong Tayiji and the king of Tsang were both patrons of the Karma Kagyu tradition, with which Jatsön himself was closely affiliated.

Included in this book are four translations: the complete autobiography; Tsele's account of Jatsön's final days; Norbu Gyenpa's account of the revelation of the *Embodiment of the Three Jewels*; and Jatsön Nyingpo's own account of his dream journey to Guru Rinpoche's realm, an extract from his Secret Memoir. For the reader's convenience, these four translations are called Part One, Part Two, and so on.

It has taken me a shameful number of years to complete this translation, but the fact that it has been finally completed is entirely due to the encouragement and blessings provided by the following people:

His Holiness the Seventeenth Karmapa Ogyen Trinley Dorje, who has blessed this project in many ways; the Lord of Refuge Kalu Rinpoche, Karma Rangjung Kunkhyap; Khenchen Thrangu Rinpoche; and Lama Norlha Rinpoche.

Peter van Deurzen and Maureen McNicholas have made this book possible by publishing and editing it. Maureen, in particular, is much more than an editor or publisher; it would be more apt to call her a creator of books. Her standards for both editing and the creation of books in general would improve the quality of books everywhere were they universally implemented.

Eric Colombel and the Tsadra Foundation have made the publication of this book financially possible. More than that, Eric's devoted commitment to the support and publication of so many aspects of dharma are an inspiration to me.

Without the Buddhist Digital Resource Center, founded by the eminent Dr. Gene Smith, I would have had no access to multiple editions of the texts translated here, and therefore no way to compare different editions in order to determine their accuracy. Beyond that, the Buddhist Digital Resource Center gives so many of us, Tibetans and non-Tibetans alike, ready access to countless Tibetan books that would otherwise be unavailable, and in many cases would probably no longer exist.

Whatever good there is in these translations is entirely due to the above mentioned people. Any and all errors are mine alone.

Yeshe Gyamtso

This translation is dedicated to the longevity and activity of His Holiness Ogyen Trinley Dorje, the Seventeenth Gyalwang Karmapa

Part One

The Outer Memoir of the Supreme Emanation, the Vidyadhara Jatsön Nyingpo

Chapter One: 1585–1626

OM AH HUM VAJRA GURU PADMA SIDDHI HUM

I prostrate to the infallible sources of refuge.

To Shakyaraja Munindra, lord of the doctrine;
Lake-Born Vajra, unstained by birth;
Chandraprabhakumara, lord of Tibet;[1]
Gyalwang Karmapa, single ornament of Jambudvipa;
And the noble lord Mipam, all Buddhas embodied:[2]
To the sources of present and future refuge, I bow with devotion.

I pray for the patience of the protectors, custodians of dharma,
With my composition of this little shastra.
Although the qualities of the victors are beyond description,

1. Chandraprabhakumara was the name of Gampopa's previous life during the time of the Buddha; here it refers to Gampopa himself.

2. Mipam refers here to Dungkar Tulku Mipam Tashi Lodrö (1577-1636), Jatsön Nyingpo's root guru.

How could someone like me have a story worth
telling?
Nevertheless, I've been repeatedly urged by those
with faith to tell it,
So I will write roughly rather than refuse.
Scholars and siddhas, may you not be displeased!

From any point of view, it is unfitting that I describe my life. Given that I have no outer, inner, or secret qualities, how could I possibly dare to write about myself? The sightless cannot lead the sightless; one drowning person cannot rescue another.

This talk of telling the story of my life all started with the physician Chonga Gönpo, who repeatedly said to me, "From your childhood onward you've had no propensity for worldly life, only for holy dharma; you're amazing! It would help many beings if you wrote a brief account of your life. Please do so!"

I replied, "There is nothing about my life worth writing about. If I were to claim things that are untrue, writing like an old charlatan, or write an account of my life praising myself based on a few dreams and deluded visions, it might please a few fools, but if any scholars or siddhas saw it they would be disgusted, and the powerful dharma protectors would certainly prevent me."

Then one day the retreat lama Tsewang Chöpel said to me, "Nowadays there is no one around here with your accomplishment, austerity, revulsion, retreat experience, wisdom, or discipline; it seems there never has been. Please dictate at least a partial account of your life; I will write it down. It will help the minds of many male and female monastics."

I replied, "Lama, it's kind of you to say that, but how could I speak of my life? I don't even know writing or composition. I've not seen many things in my life. I've not traveled widely. I've not spent much time in monasteries. I've never studied; I'm hardly learned. My best qualities are to have never had trouble with sex or alcohol; to have never parted from the three dharma robes; to have spent time in strict retreat; to diligently mumble my way through liturgical dharma practices; to recite mantras; and to have familiarized myself with tranquility meditation as best I could. My diligence in dharma consists of those alone. It would be pointless to write an account of my life! Not only is there nothing praiseworthy to write about; it might cause the accumulation of negative karma through exaggerated and dismissive gossip."

Then a few monks who are my friends said, "From the time you were in your mother's womb until now there have been many amazing signs. Even now you continue to remain in retreat and nourish yourself solely through rasayana.[3.] There are many tales of your miracles and supercognition. We really need at least a brief account of your life."

I dealt with some of these requests by pretending to get angry, with some by patiently refusing, and with some by saying, "Not now. If I'm still alive at the age of fifty-five, I'll tell my story then."

3. Rasayana is the yogic discipline of deriving nourishment solely from minerals, herbs, air, or awareness.

Later, when I reached Bangri Tashi Öbar, several people said to me, "Your songs and instructions are many; a brief account of your life is absolutely needed! Please write a brief life story including a prayer to your previous births."

Many people made this request. I replied, "How could I possibly remember my previous births? The victors of the past had perfect wisdom, love, and ability. As the signs of their internal perfection were externally evident through the interdependence of the external and internal, every line of memoir or song they wrote could turn the minds of many people to holy dharma. As they had control over the five elements, they could please all beings. They remembered their own previous births, and knew the minds of others.

"We use their example as an excuse to turn ourselves into dharma charlatans! We pretend to have accomplished what we haven't, to have destroyed delusion that we haven't, to have practiced what we haven't, to have realized equal taste when we haven't, and to be able to digest donations that we can't. We do our best to fool people. We exchange our welfare in future lives for one day's worth of food and drink. For the sake of even one thing we want we abandon holy dharma. When we drink alcohol we act worse than demons. We would kill even our parents for a morsel of tasty food. We denigrate the Buddha's stainless teachings whenever we fail to get everything we want. When we're displeased we turn our backs on the three jewels, and if we succeed in acquiring even a needle and some thread we thank the gods. If we spend even three days in retreat we think we're amazing. What we really are, however, is heaps of defects mired in a swamp of kleshas. We are blindfolded by ignorance and bound by the ropes of the five poisons. We can't even control our minds for the amount of time it takes to drink one cup of tea; each thought leads to another like the links of a chain. When I think of all this, I want to weep all day and night. Even if I wrote an account of my life it would be unlikely to help anyone. It would be like a fox attempting to leap in the wake of a tiger."

Later, the omniscient Drukchen and the supreme nirmanakaya of Daklha Gampo said to me, "When the story of someone's life is wondrous, it should not be allowed to sink into oblivion. Write down some notes; we will edit them for you afterward. It would be fitting for us to tell your story." Many other holy beings also said much the same thing.

Finally, a few clever people asked, "May we write your life story in brief?"

I replied, "You may not. The victor Yungtönpa said:

> Most accounts of gurus' lives written by disciples
> Overpraise the gurus, turning them into charlatans.
> You know yourself best; write it yourself.

And Lord Barawa said:

> Although it seems unfitting to write an account of
> your own life,

If others do it they will fill it with meaningless
obsequiousness."

If I therefore write a scattered and rough account in words no better than the bleating of goats and sheep, may genuine scholars, siddhas, and those with eyes of wisdom not be displeased. In particular, I pray that the stern protectors ensure the absence of obstacles.

Guru, think of me! Three jewels, think of me! Great Padmakara of Uddiyana, think of me! Dharma king Physician from Dakpo, think of me! Noble lord Mipam Lodrö, think of me! Grant your blessings so that this may help beings!

If I briefly set forth my outer, inner, and secret memoirs, now is not the time to write my secret memoir. My inner memoir is already contained within the large collection of my songs. I will therefore write a brief account of my outer life.

4. Chökyong Gönpo means "Dharma-Protecting Lord."

My father was called Chökyong Gönpo.[4] He once dreamed that he was exploring a hidden valley called Uddiyana Gorge. Between two mountains he found a temple containing an extremely large image of Guru Padma surrounded by many images wearing the Dakpo Kagyu meditation hat. Many people were presenting fine offerings to them.

He also dreamed that he created a large spring on the mountain behind Dingtang by thrusting a khatvanga into the ground. There was a loud roar, and then he heard a voice shouting, "Hear this! Hear this! There is no longer the need to speak of dry Dingtang! No one's ever seen a spring greater than this one!"

He later told me that as these dreams occurred while my mother was pregnant with me, he took them to be about me.

My mother was called Namlang Butri.[5] She repeatedly dreamed that within her was a ball of light, like an inflated placenta, that was very smooth and as shiny as water, giving forth the sound of OM AH HUM.

5. Namlang Butri means "Dawn of Sons."

She also dreamed that while walking on a road she found a crystal stupa and a yellow mala. She too took her dreams to be about the child in her womb.

During her pregnancy she was never ill, and all her dreams were of ganachakras and of many books of scripture. Namtsal Trungpa Sönam Gyamtso told her, "The child in your womb is extraordinary." His statement was later credited as precognition.

Several neighbors in our village saw rainbows ending at our house and many other signs.

I was born under the constellation Pushya in the Female Wood Bird Year, in a protector temple at a site where both the sky and the ground were triangular.

They say that as I was being born there was at first thunder, lightning, a brief hailstorm, an earthquake, a windstorm, and an eerie sound filling the sky, so that everyone was terrified. Then, after a little while, the sun emerged and the whole sky was filled with rainbow clouds and a pleasant fragrance.

The bhikshu who was the lama of the protector temple

reportedly said, "What is this child? Today was terrifying, what with that earthquake and all!" He gave me a hundred permission-blessings of the Six-Armed Mahakala and the name Gyalwa Gönpo. Later my name was changed by Lama Uma Rechen to Chapkar Gyalpo.[6]

My mother told me of many wondrous signs she witnessed in experiences and dreams around the time of my birth, but I'm not going to write of them here.

In my third year I reportedly learned to read just by being shown the letters; I have no memory of learning the alphabet.

6. Gyalwa Gönpo means "Victorious Protector"; Chapkar Gyalpo means "King of White Water."

In my fifth year I began to remain awake at night. During the night I often heard a continuous ringing in both my ears. Listening to it, I would feel intensely sad and unhappy. Repeatedly listening to the sound brought up, beyond my control, the thought of death. Both my parents were invariably sound asleep.

I continuously had the thought, "I wish I could meet Gampopa right now!" Constantly in my mind was the image of a thin elderly bhikshu, wearing a somewhat dirty dharma robe, with a light complexion. I would recite OM MANI PADME HUM many times, keeping him in mind.

As an infant I insisted on sleeping in my father's lap and would not stay put in my mother's arms.

I would reportedly urge people to recite MANIs and was clever at making up and singing songs. All of my childish play was the imitation of writing, drawing, sculpting, setting up offerings, and drawing mandalas. I often pretended to be in retreat, hiding under the roof, in the grass, between columns, and in culverts. I reportedly often went to wherever there were no people, such as inside hollow trees or caves, and sat in the posture and gaze of meditation. I would fall asleep there and someone would have to go looking for me. The habit of gazing into space with open eyes is one I've maintained from infancy down to the present day.

I also pretended to give empowerments to my childhood friends, as well as teach them dharma and enlist their aid in building temples. I would get them to build thrones for me out of stone on which they would pile their coats; then they would prostrate to me. When I taught them dharma and had them repeat the refuge after me, a few elderly people wept, saying, "Such a child has never been seen!" Everyone in our village agreed that I must be the rebirth of a good lama.

I recounted vague recollections of a few previous lives, but my parents kept this secret. I refused to eat meat or garlic. They say that even the way I walked, ate, and dressed displayed good habits unlearned in this life.

I could immediately stop dust storms and rainstorms merely through my gaze and pointed forefinger. On many occasions I was able to exorcize spirits and heal children afflicted by spirits just by blowing on them; that I remember myself. I take this as a sign that I engaged in sadhana in previous lives. Because of this I was given the nicknames Bhikshu and Mahasiddha by our neighbors.

From the age of six to eleven I would follow monks around whenever I could, with a desire to enter a monastery as intense as a thirsty person's desire for water. However, as I was the child of ordinary folk, my parents refused to let me go. I felt so sad about this that I wept day and night. When I was sent off to herd pigs and protect our fields from rodents, I became extremely depressed and lost any attachment I might have had to our land. I remember thinking, "It would have been better to be born the child of beggars than this!"

I was so depressed that I was incapable of doing much work. I would have enjoyed study, but my parents didn't permit it.

In those days whenever I saw a statue, painting, or book I would experience overwhelming joy. When I had the opportunity to pick up a vajra, bell, or damaru I would be so delighted that I would forget to eat. Whenever I saw male or female monastics or hermits I felt more affection for them than I did for even my own parents. When such persons left for another area I would weep uncontrollably. Feeling terribly sad, I would think, "When will I escape my birthplace?"

Sometimes I went where there were no other people and prostrated to the eight directions, praying, "Gurus and the three jewels, with your eyes of wisdom you must see my misery! I pray that you care for me compassionately so that I be able to practice true dharma!"

Sometimes I repeatedly and desperately called to Guru Padma with the thought, "How unfortunate am I to have been born in this miserable region!" In those days many verses of prayer issued spontaneously from my lips. They were meaningless but frequent, and consisted of things like "I am devoted to the gods of the elements." I also called a number of colorful rocks deities and filled our house with them.

Whenever I got hold of any butter I would use it to make offering lamps. On every holy day I would say, "We should perform a ganachakra." I would imitate the melodies and liberation offerings used in such ceremonies, recite mantras of exhortation, and pretend to throw tormas. I didn't know a single word of any liturgy, but I certainly had good habits formed in previous lives.

When I recited mantras I would hear many other people reciting them too, as though they were actually there. When itinerant tantrikas came to recite rituals, and when lamas came to recite scriptures, I managed to memorize a few words here and there and gained a good understanding of them. This influenced everyone around me; they became slightly more concerned with dharma. Even my parents began to acknowledge that their son was unusual. As I had slight supercognition and minor miraculous abilities they worried that I would have a short life.

Eventually I was sent off to learn writing and calligraphy. Soon after that I met the Ninth Gyalwang Karmapa Wangchuk Dorje and felt faith unlike anything I had felt before. Even now, I can see his face as clearly as if he were right here.

His great disciple, Yangri Trungpa Sönam Zangpo, gave protection knots to my parents and told them,

"Allow your little boy to practice holy dharma! If you won't, have him study medicine for the time being. In the end, though, he will practice dharma." He blessed me with his hand and voiced good aspirations for me.

This caused my faith to increase even more. Weeping, I prayed to him, saying, "Please care for me!"

He replied, "In the end, you will definitely practice holy dharma," and nodded his head. Gazing at me intensely, he then said, "AI! KARMAPA KHYENNO!" He gave me some samaya substance pills and a protection knot. I received from him the *Single Deity Single Vase Ayusadhana* empowerment and the transmission of the mantra OM MANI PADME HUM. I gained genuine devotion for that guru, but didn't have much faith in most of those I met in those days. Because I am very proud and arrogant, I have not offered prostrations to or had faith in many people. I suppose this could be a habit stemming from being somewhat spoiled by my parents.

Soon after that I went to study medicine, which I did for the next nine years. I studied the three tantras, the three compositions, the summaries, the commentaries, the definitive instructions, and the great expositions; and was trained in the examination of pulses and blood. During the summers I gathered and prepared herbal medicines. In the mornings I memorized treatises and was examined each afternoon. I wrote down my own notes on the most important medical procedures. During breaks I would recite mantras, and even when I was reciting treatises to commit them to memory I would first recite the vow of refuge, the generation of bodhichitta, the seven branches, a prayer to Guru Rinpoche, and a praise of Gampopa. I prayed, "May everyone who hears my voice be helped greatly! May they be drawn to holy dharma!"

Perhaps because of my compassionate intention, people would gather to listen to me recite my medical textbooks. This caused a few young people to turn to holy dharma, brought some elderly people to tears, and encouraged many to recite the MANI mantra. As I had a pleasant voice I was able to please everyone, young or old, but the whole time I was thinking, "Training to be a physician like this is just learning a way to support myself." I had no real enthusiasm for my studies. I secretly memorized the *Ornament of Precious Liberation*, the *Precious Garland of the Supreme Path*, the *Self-Liberation of Habits*, and the *Seven Chapters*.[7] When my medical teacher found out he beat me and scolded me at length. He threw my meal bag and bedding off a cliff, saying, "I don't care where you go, but leave!"

This all left me incredibly depressed. My frustrated desire to practice dharma made me as sad as a mother whose only child has died. I continued, however, to recite my medical texts from memory to my medical teacher, and recite the *Ornament of Liberation* and the other books secretly. Whenever I had a moment to think I would pray, "May I have the opportunity to practice holy dharma!" It was around then that a number of signs began to repeatedly appear in my dreams and

7. The *Ornament of Precious Liberation* is Gampopa's best known work. The *Precious Garland of the Supreme Path* is also by Gampopa. The *Self Liberation of Habits* is a terma of Karma Lingpa. The *Seven Chapters* are prayers to Guru Rinpoche.

hypnagogic experiences and I began to compose many verses of liturgy; I burned them later.

I was very careful to be clean and to wash, and was quite concerned with contagion and impurity. Whenever I saw a large gathering of people in those days I would think, "Every one of these people will be dead within a hundred years! This is all like a dream or magical illusion!," and feel a sharp sadness in my heart. My parents were getting old by this time, and were not wealthy. I had to support us by reading scriptures in people's homes, by performing cleansing smoke offering ceremonies, and by preparing herbal medicine.

Many people died then because of an outbreak of cholera. This increased my sadness; I felt a deep revulsion for worldly life as intense as the disgust that would be felt by a nauseated person if food were placed in front of them. Since that time I have never felt the slightest interest in sex.

In my fifteenth year I was able to save the lives of eleven people who were close to death from a fever that also caused intestinal cramps. I also saved the lives of many beggars and starving people. I had great compassion in those days, and was diligent in liturgical recitation. Since the age of thirteen I have never neglected the daily recitation of the *Five Royal Sutras*, both White and Green Tara, a number of longevity dharanis equal to my years, a thousand MANIs, and the hundredfold torma offering.[8]

In my sixteenth year an obstacle arose which caused

8. The *Five Royal Sutras* are the *Aspiration to Excellent Conduct*, the sutra of aspiration; the *Vajravidarana Dharani*, the sutra of ablution; the *Heart of the Perfection of Wisdom*, the sutra of the view; *Wisdom at Passing*, the sutra of meditation; and the *Sutra of Three Sections*, the sutra of confession.

me to have a bad dream that left me uncomfortable. I developed a skin disease that included abscesses, swellings, and discoloration of the skin, and had many dreams about nagas. Since it seemed I had been poisoned by an earthlord, I requested a Vajrapani empowerment and transmission from a lama and recited the mantra a great deal. I also offered naga tormas and prayed to both Guru Padma and the peerless Gampopa. I said to my medical teacher, "Whether due to past karma or present circumstances, I am unhappy. I want only to practice holy dharma, but it seems that this obstacle is going to cause my death. My elderly parents are extremely sad."

When I told him this I began to weep uncontrollably, and my teacher also shed tears. He tried to console me in various ways, but I was inconsolable, unable to think clearly. I went somewhere where there were no people and remained there, weeping. Eventually I summoned up my courage and resumed mantra recitation and meditation focused on my illness.

More than a year later I dreamed that I killed a dog and that I exuded a lot of insects, pus, and blood from my big toes and anus. After that I recovered, but I continued the Vajrapani mantra accumulation until I eventually reached one hundred million. All this enabled me to significantly help others as well; my own illness caused me to feel spontaneous compassion for others.

Then my parents were separated by the death of my father, who had been ill for a long time. I had been treating him assiduously, both medically and through interdependence, but was unable to help him much. After his breathing stopped and before his circulation ceased altogether I read him the *Liberation Through Hearing* and recited the names of buddhas. After three days of praying for him I cremated him and made satsas out of his bones. I continued to recite the Buddha's words and present offerings weekly for his benefit.

I dreamed that my father said to me, "Oh, this passage of the bardo is long! I am afraid! I am afraid! Continue to recite the *Stainless Confession Tantra* and the *Liberation Through Hearing*!" I added samaya substances to a good singed offering fire and recited aspirations and the *Stainless Confession Tantra*. After twenty days I dreamed that my father said to me, "I am going to be born a human boy!"

Soon after that I said to my mother, "Father is gone. My brother is still young, but if you two lack food, sell your field and feed yourselves with what you get for it. As for me, I can think of nothing other than holy dharma; I am going to spend the rest of my life living in austerity, surviving on water alone." My mother responded to this declaration in various ways, depending on her mood. Sometimes she seemed delighted by my intentions; at other times she wept and argued with me. She also engaged in a number of strategic attempts to marry me off, which was her real hope. This led to constant quarreling between us, mother and son, all day and night. I was repeatedly brought to tears, as was my mother.

We fought over this for two months. Then my father's

house was destroyed by a torrential rain. That evening, while I was trying desperately to save it, I heard the mournful bleating of goats and sheep; the sound left me unbearably depressed. Seeing married home life amid these dregs of time as a fire pit or dungeon, I knew that there was no opportunity in it for happiness. Whenever I saw juniper forests, grassy or rocky mountains, or isolated hermitages surrounded by wafting mists I felt intense joy, contentment, and enthusiasm.

For the time being I regularly performed five- and seven-day-long fasts and performed the *Sutra Ritual of Baishajyaguru* a hundred times. I repeatedly practiced the sadhana of Vajrapani and was diligent in liturgical practices and mantra repetition. I made fervent and vast aspirations at all the sacred sites in Kongpo from Gyala onward, especially White Rock Divine Water and Three Rock Lake, and at all the temples in the area. My prayer was that I soon be able to live a life devoted exclusively to holy dharma.

At the time I came to believe that Norbu Gyenpa, the supreme nirmanakaya of Daklha Gampo, had been my guru during many lifetimes. I also understood that it would be wondrously good to enter the presence of the Karmapa and his dharma sons. However, I thought that given their elevated status as gurus with so many disciples I would not be able to receive detailed, experiential instruction from them; and that I would therefore lack the necessary guidance.

Throughout the day and night I thought about

whether there were any qualified gurus from whom I could request dharma in my area, and came to the conclusion that there were none. There were some lamas with learning, even erudition, and with the appearance of monastic discipline, but they were all avaricious and greedy. There were other lamas with the appearance of accomplishment through practice and the observance of strict retreat, but they had little learning and seemed incapable of teaching. Some lamas appeared impure, given their heedless consumption of offerings given to them on behalf of the living and dead. I saw others who, fallen under the sway of alcohol and sex, were no different than worldly folk. I felt that some, because of their youth, might be untrustworthy in the long term in spite of their apparent goodness. I was also afraid that if I had to travel to a distant area to study my mother would be devastated, and I might be unable to return at the time of her death.

No matter how I thought about it, I had great difficulty in coming to a decision. I was wary of becoming one of those who wander from village to village, drinking beer as they go, and sinking themselves ever further into the swamp of samsara.

In my twenty-first year I began to think, "What if I enter the presence of the precious dharma lord Mipam Tashi Lodrö?"

I prayed to the three jewels. As I had good dreams about doing so, I entered his presence without hesitation. He cut my hair and made me a shramanera. I received instruction on mahamudra from him, and began to memorize some of the ceremonies and liturgies of the Drukpa tradition.

I remember thinking at that time, upon careful consideration, "I will not study. If I wanted to study, I could do that anywhere. I will focus on emulating the practice style of Naga Kachu, feeding myself with rasayana, wearing whatever garments come to me, avoiding human company, and not letting any offerings to the sangha enter my mouth."

While I was living in Sheltö, I wrote this praise of the area:

NAMO GURU AJITAMATIYE![9]
Lord, precious guide of all beings,
Please send me the light rays of your love.

To the south of the central highest mountain,
To the north of Vajrasana,
To the east of Shakyamuni's image,[10]
To the west of Bhakha in Kongpo,
Below the meeting point of two rock faces
Is a place predicted by the peerless physician
Gampopa.

Above a rock like piled jewels
Its site is auspicious and splendid, with fine features.
Our lord forefathers called it
Sheltö Bower of the Gods.

9. Ajitamati is Mipam Lodrö in Sanskrit. Ajitamatiye means "To Ajitamati."

10. Shakyamuni's image refers here to the Jokang in Lhasa.

Its fame now fills the ten directions.
It has revealed the profound treasure of dharma.
In its glorious, luminous hall of accomplishment
My father lord of dharma, my source of refuge,
Placed his form on the unchanging lion throne.

His speech continuously turned the mahayana dharmachakra,
His mind immersed in the equality of spontaneous presence.
He was surrounded by many bodhisattvas on the levels.
He rained down the torrential dharma of sutra and tantra.
He brought our mothers, all beings, to the path of liberation.
He brought all with karmic connection to joy.
He changed everyone who saw or heard him and brought them to dharma.
We who are devoted to him are fortunate.

Anyone who wants supreme or common siddhi:
Be devoted to this community of accomplishment!
Through the blessings of our father Kagyu gurus,
The power of infallible cause and result,
And the truth of my good intentions,
May the teachings long remain in this place.

– Written at Sheltö Bower of the Gods.

Then, I next undertook the vows of completion in the presence of the peerless Lhatse Rinpoche, from whom I also received numerous transmissions, including the *Biography of Lorepa*, and many empowerments and instructions. The first empowerments and the first dharma I received from the precious lord of dharma were the empowerments of Amitayus and Hayagriva. The first transmissions I received from him were the biographies of Lingrepa and Tsangpa Gyare, the protector of beings. I also received from him the empowerments from the *Vajramala*, the *Ocean of Sadhanas*, the *Hundred Instructions of the Severance Master Sangye Pal*, the collected writings of most of the Kagyu gurus, the *Buddha's Lives*, the collected writings of the dharma king Songtsen Gampo, many Nyingma teachings, and all the instructions of the Drukpa tradition. I also received other entrustments and authorizations. Most of these are recorded in my *Account of Teachings Received*. I also received many dharmapala cycles.

The dharma lord Mipam Tashi Lodrö was extremely kind to me; I in turn perceived him as a buddha. To this day, whatever I do, I first pray to Guru Padma and the dharma lord Mipam Tashi Lodrö; this has brought the accomplishment of my every wish. Although I do not have a lot of food or wealth, I am happy, I think, because I am free. From the time when my heart first turned to dharma until today my pillow has always supported books of dharma. My efforts in the memorization and review of these texts have been inexhaustible; I have pushed myself to the point of irritation. I hope that this has purified wrongs and veils.

Other gurus with whom I have formed a dharma connection include the Ninth Karmapa Wangchuk Dorje, who is my guru in that I saw, heard, and continue to recollect him; the Tenth Karmapa Chöying Dorje, with whom I have formed a dharma connection; Garwang Chökyi Wangchuk, the sixth holder of the red crown, from whom I received transmissions for meditation on guruyoga and Avalokita; Gyaltsap Rinpoche, from whom I received much dharma including *Amitāyus: the Combined Sādhana of the Three Roots*; the omniscient Drukpa, from whom I received the *Wrathful Guru of Lord Nyang*; Norbu Gyenpa, the supreme nirmanakaya of Daklha Gampo, from whom I received Gampopa's collected writings, the collected writings of Dakpo Tashi Namgyal, the *Wish-Fulfilling Jewel: Guidance on the Mind*, the *Scroll of the Protector Trakshad*, and many other teachings; Yangri Trungpa Sönam Zangpo, from whom I received a longevity empowerment and a MANI transmission; Latö Jangdak Tashi Topgyal, from whom I received an explanation of the benefits of the tenth-day observance and a Peaceful Guru empowerment; the great abbot of Joden, from whom I received a Baishajyaguru authorization and much other dharma; Lama Tsewang Chöpel, from whom I received the *Eight Dispensations of Nyang*, the *Liberation through*

Hearing of Ayupati Yamantaka, the *Assembly of Samantabhadra's Wisdom*, *Penetrating Wisdom*, *Guru Guhyasamaja*, and much other dharma; Tsele Tulku Natsok Rangdröl, from whom I received the *Eight Dispensations: The Complete Secrets*, the termas of Guru Chöwang, the *General Tantra of Piled Lotuses*, the *Hot Red Cord of Mantra*, the empowerment of the *Vajramala Ayusadhana*, and other teachings; the master Damchö Puntsok, from whom I received the entrustments of the *Hundred Teachings of Mitra* and of all of the Nyingma teachings he had received; the dharma practitioner Ngaki Wangpo, from whom I received the burning and reversal rituals of *Yamantaka Khalamebar* and other teachings; Jakyungpa Gyalwang Tendzin, from whom I received the transmission-empowerment from the *Wisdom Assembly of the Guru*; Ngakchang Tashi Tseten, from whom I received many teachings including the *Play of the Wrathful Ones* along with its reversal rituals; and the mahasiddha Tendzin Dorje, from whom I received the Drikung *Single Intention*, the collected works of Lord Rinchen Puntsok, and the *Utterly Profound Intention*.

I've also formed dharma connections with other lamas of high, intermediate, and low standing. From Lama Nangta Dorje I received the *Nine Heart-Essence Cycles*, the biographies of the successive hierarchs of the Karma Kagyu, and the Karma Kagyu *Five-Deity Vajravarahi*. From the bhikshu Karma Tashi, a holy heart-son of the

Ninth Karmapa Wangchuk Dorje, I received the complete reading transmission of the *Translated Words of the Buddha*; the Karma Kagyu *Mahakala, Jinasagara,* and *Vajravarahi*; the collected writings of the successive hierarchs of that tradition; and many other transmissions and instructions. In all, I have relied on forty-eight lamas and masters.

I have stayed in all sorts of places, including Daklha Gampo, Dröchen, Dröchung, Tsaritra, Tsagong, Tölung Tsurphu, Densatil, Drikung, Lhasa, Samye, Chimpu, Tsanang Gyala, Sengam, Tsojuk, Buchu Jongka, Nampu Gangra, Puri, Bapang Hermitage, Tsojong, Midu Divine Rock, Lama Place, the upper valley of Olma Six Lakes, Duri, Polek Nganang, Dorje Drak, Kartse End, Pangbu Gangra, Menmo Draktsa, the cave of Sangye Lingpa at Pangbu, Nyangdam Retreat, Sheltö Bower of the Gods, the Cave of Spirits, Riu Cave, Softwater Spring, and other caves, wooden huts, shelters, and ruins.

In such places I depended on rasayana for nourishment and a worn-out shawl for clothing. Without any preferences regarding whatever appeared I sustained unaltered relaxation and tried to mix day and night. In that way I exerted myself to the best of my ability.

In my twenty-fifth year I entered closed retreat at Softwater Spring, and remained in retreat for around seventeen years. During those years I achieved a few qualities of experience and realization and wrote this praise of that place:

NAMO GURU AJITAMATIYE!
Mipam Lodrö, holy lord, my only refuge, hear me!
This place, Bangri Jokpo, was blessed by Guru Rinpoche.
High and majestic, its virtues are indescribable.

Its snow-covered peak is like a stupa of crystal.
Its base stands on a changeless vajra ground.
Between them is the vivid display of gods and goddesses.
Its top is the palace of Mahakarunika.

It has seven golden mountains, seven pools, and a hundred caves
Where Padma practiced and left a hundred handprints.
The deities seen in visions here are as numerous as stars in the sky.

The rock to this mountain's right is called Chudo;
It displays the array of viras and kimkaras.
To its left are Dingpo and Dingmo,
Luminous realms of the dakinis of the three levels.
In front is Hom Gorge Iron Gate,
Even more awe-inspiring than the rock mountains of dharmapalas.
Atop it is a wondrous white vase.
It is this land's eye, where the six realms' veils can be purified.
Behind it are a sacred, holy lake and swamp,

Brimming with the blessings of all victors.

This place's guardian is Dorje Draktsen, who accomplishes
My and others' activity according to Padma's command.
Especially, in this place Softwater Spring,
Where samadhi arises of itself,
Beneath a rock like a bejeweled box
Flows a stream of milk, dispelling kleshas.

Surrounded by junipers, the best of trees,
I sit with legs crossed in my little square hut,
Nourishing myself with flower essences.
Beautiful songs flow steadily from my lips.

Above, ptarmigans send forth their calls.
Below, larks call sweetly.
In between, swans speak in varied ways.
Dharmic friends pray melodiously.

On sacred days fragrant incense fills the air,
Sounds of music come from the sky,
And rainbow clouds gather in the shape of many deities.
I continuously dream of dakinis gathering.

This place is for now a hidden Buddha.
If anyone remembers holy dharma, they should come here.

> Through the virtue of writing this, may my activity be vast.

I wrote many other songs as well. From the age of twenty, until my thirty-seventh year, neither meat nor alcohol passed my lips. I nourished myself with dolomite, eating only once a day. I mostly relied solely on rasayana and on air. I used only one measure of tea leaves every three days; I would drink tea made from it on the first day, reuse the same leaves for two more days, and then eat the leaves on the third day. I used whatever butter was offered me to make offering lamps, stretching each of those out for three days as well. I used whatever cloth was given me to make prayer flags on which I wrote MANI mantras. I maintained verbal silence throughout sacred days during both the waxing and waning phases of each lunar month; combined together, I estimate that I spent a total of seven years in silence. On the fifteenth thirtieth, eighth, tenth, twenty-fifth, and twenty-ninth days of each month I performed many different mandala rituals. When I first began my retreat I performed a hundred thousand prostrations, a hundred thousand hundred-syllable mantras, a hundred thousand mandala offerings, a hundred thousand prayers, and a hundred thousand aspirations. Extremely clear signs of purification arose. I continued to perform a hundred of each of these practices daily.

After completing those preliminaries I began the practice of chandali, starting with the empty enclosure;

bliss and heat blazed greatly. Each day I continuously practiced a great deal of both the intermediate breathing and mantra repetition.

One day I observed from my retreat a lot of people engaged in plowing and burning fields. I sang to them:

NAMO GURU AJITAMATIYE!
Only refuge from samsara's three realms,
Lord of compassion Avalokiteshvara,
Inseparable from my guru, the lord of dharma,
Gaze compassionately upon beings in these
dregs of time!

I, a young monk born at the end of time,
Am speaking to you having felt for you in my heart.
Most human beings of the present seem to have
Fallen into their state rather than gained it.

Dharma friends are as rare as daytime stars.
The land is filled with demonic people.
With human bodies they act like beasts.
They devote their lives to wrongdoing
Without ever getting enough food or clothing.
Their future destination will be a lower state.

Oh, oh, what can I do?
Oh, my parents, beings of the six states
Untamed by past victors,
You are going to suffer for a long time.

There is no way to change ripened karma.

In this miserable prison of samsara,
You become deluded in your youth
And drink the poisonous water of attachment and anger.

You regret this once you're old, but what good does that do?
Jealous of the high, you revile the low
And compete with your equals.
Oh, oh, what can I do?

Given the short lives of those who practice dharma
And the apparent merit of evil leaders,
It seems unlikely that beings will ever be happy.
They deceive one another in this abyss of samsara,
Like a bag of beans spilling out.

Guru, three jewels, care for them with compassion!
I too have no idea where I'm going;
There's nothing to be done about it, but I can't stand it!
May all beings reach liberation through virtue!

I wrote many such songs; they may be found in my *Collected Songs*.

During that time I completed the mantra repetition of many yidams, dakinis, and dharmapalas. I performed hundredfold fulfillment and confession many times. Ever since then I have regretted my previous wrong-doing and, with the intention of creating a good remedy for it, have offered my body, speech, and mind to the three jewels. I continue to regard whatever happens to me, whether good or bad, as the three jewels' kindness. Everything I do is done for the benefit of beings, my parents; I am committed to never acting selfishly. I have learned to trust myself in this at least.

At that time I witnessed many signs in actuality, hypnagogia, and dreams. I was accepted by Guru Padma, and signs of it being time for me to reveal profound terma appeared, but I will not write of that here; let's leave that aside for now.[11]

11. This refers to the events leading up to Jatsön's discovery of the *Embodiment of the Three Jewels*. Although his reference to it here is enigmatic, its place in the text appears to support the dating of that revelation to 1608 C.E.

I made many promises to myself, such as spending all four sessions in the seven dharmas of Vairochana; and performing a hundred refuge vows, bodhisattva vows, hundred-syllable mantras, mandala offerings, and supplications every session. I didn't lie down at night, and mostly depended on an austere regimen of rasayana for nourishment. I mixed whatever I could find among rhododendron flowers, calcite, dolomite, Solomon's seal, juniper berries, ever-weeping flower, and *Orchis latifolia* in a soup with roots, greens, daikon, and turnips. I once lived solely on the rasayana of prana and awareness for two and a half years. I kept nothing extra, and had no knives or weapons. In all, I lived as an actionless yogin for about seventeen years.

My body became weak. I had trouble sleeping at night. When rain fell at dusk, when I heard thunder or saw the flash of lightning, or whenever I felt delusion overtaking my perception I would think, "Oh, this night some people are suffering from unbearable sickness and pain. Others are oppressed by the suffering of fighting and quarreling. Some are controlled by their search for food and drink. Some are beating their breasts in mourning. Most are deeply asleep. Many who have previously gathered the accumulations are living alone in isolated hermitages, praying loudly, free from acceptance and rejection, natural and relaxed, resting in self-aware wisdom. Most others are wasting their lives. All these beings have been my kind parents, yet I have been unable to do them any significant good; I place my hopes in mere aspirations for distant benefit. Guru, three jewels, help!"

Thinking in such a way once caused my prana to get stuck in my upper body; for three days I found it difficult to breathe. At night, all my dreams were of the bardo and of Yama Dharmarajah, who held a khatvanga and mirror and wore a meditation hat and a golden brocade dharma robe blazing with light. He was the size of Varuna Yepa Mountain, and was accompanied by a vast number of other yamas. The environment in those dreams was without mountains, a great plain of sand. All the water was as red as blood. When I climbed a hill I saw a huge crowd of all sorts of people, animals, and other beings, all loudly speaking their respective tongues. Seeing all this, I became terrified and dizzy. Many of the human men and women I saw spoke to me in their various dialects and gave me messages to bring back to their parents, children, and other relatives, whom they mentioned by name. Their messages ran,

"Help, help! We have no hope other than you!"

They were all weeping, making enough noise to fill the galaxy. I couldn't help myself; I started to weep too.

After those dreams began I wept day and night, and throughout the day I was overcome by what I had seen in my dreams. Having no idea what to do, an ocean of misery burst forth within me. Sleeping didn't help; getting back up didn't help. No matter what I did, such as walking or sitting, nothing helped. This lasted about a week.

I began to think that I should leave retreat. I took medicine for prana illness, ate nutritious food, applied ointments, and diligently practiced the techniques that help in such cases. My condition improved and then, finally, I was better.

Had I not gotten better when I did, I think I would either have died then or gone seriously mad. I know that I was only cured through the kindness of my guru and the three jewels.

Soon after that male and female monastics began to gather around me, at first one or two, then seven or eight, then around twenty, and then a group of monastics and laity consisting of around forty people. I gave them empowerments and dharma instructions through the opening in my otherwise sealed retreat. There were always at least thirty people gathered there, including people practicing tranquility meditation, those practicing prostrations, MANI repeaters, ejection practitioners, people memorizing liturgies and rituals, people learning to read and write, people seeking the refuge vow, and those requesting longevity empowerments or protection rituals.

I began to think, "All these men and women living together is going to lead to a lot of married ex-monastics. If I moved to an empty valley uninhabited by anyone, entered a strict retreat, and recited aspiration prayers that would do beings more good than this."

At the same time I heard that my mother was dying, so I went to her; she died with her head pillowed in my lap. I performed the ejection of consciousness and recited dedications and aspirations. I placed a liberation-through-wearing yantra on her body and placed samaya substances in her mouth. I cremated her myself. For seven weeks I dedicated virtue to her. During those weeks I repeatedly met her in dreams; I would say to her, "Meditate on Avalokita. Repeat the MANI. Let your mind rest naturally, without alteration."

During the first week she replied, "That is not easy; I don't trust myself. My awareness is vague and indistinct; it has no stability. I have seen no happiness in this world, only suffering. My son, do whatever you can to help me!"

During the second week I dreamed that she was as real as when alive. I taught her dharma to clarify the bardo state as before, and she replied, "Oh father! Oh mother! I had no idea the bardo was going to be like this! All the people who don't practice dharma during their lives are foolish, foolish! Guru! Three jewels! When I look up I see penetrating light rays and hear empty sound. When I look down I am terrified and hear wails of agony. I have no control over what I do now. Please keep trying to help me!"

I offered a lot of butter lamps, enlisted the help of the three jewels, and made singed offerings including samaya substances; my mother was reborn as an animal.

Having witnessed what she had gone through I realized how much good I was doing myself by practicing dharma. I wrote many songs then out of sadness. I repeatedly sponsored tea service for all those staying at Softwater Spring; distributed grain, salt, and butter, and gave them whatever ragged clothing I had to give; gave barley meal and other food to starving villagers; protected the area from blights and hail; caused rainfall; prevented sickness and epidemics; protected the area from predators; gave medicine to the sick; gave yantras for eating and wearing to those who mistook their own thoughts to be demons; gave authorizations and blessings; and banished obstructors. With the best intentions, I really did whatever I could to help everyone in the area.

Most of the signs that it was time for me to reveal profound terma occurred, especially the prophesied sky sign, the flight of white birds, which lasted for two years and was seen by everyone.

Then I began to receive repeated invitations from Daklha Gampo Monastery, and my promised years of retreat were soon to be completed. To the thirty or so young monks and nuns who had gathered around me I repeatedly said, "Practice dharma earnestly; we will not always be together. I am going to leave for the mountains where there are no people and remain in strictly silent retreat. You should ask any questions you have now."

When my years of retreat ended I prepared to go to Daklha Gampo. Before going I gave empowerments, authorizations, and instruction to around eighty people.

At Daklha Gampo I first offered the transmission of profound terma to the precious dharma lord Mipam Tashi Lodrö, and then to all my brothers there, led by the supreme nirmanakaya Dakpo Norbu Gyenpa. I later offered empowerment and dharma to the Gyalwang Karmapa, father and sons; the Drikung Shapdrung and his disciples; the superior of Nedong; Lhagyal Riwa; the abbot of Tsongdü Draka; and the omniscient Drukpa.

I taught dharma to groups of around five hundred people at Jampa Chöling, Sangak Chöling, Taktse Drupde, and Podrang Yangtse. To Jarpa Tripön, his consort, children, and entourage I offered the *Ocean of Sadhanas* and the empowerments, transmissions, and instructions for profound terma along with an amrita accomplishment, and also performed a torma reversal and other services. Invited by the dharma lord Gyalwang Kukye, I gave empowerments and transmissions at Buchu Lungpa and performed a little samaya substance accomplishment there. I revealed profound terma at the Buchu Temple. Then I went to Druk Chöding, where I formed a dharma connection with about a thousand people. Invited by the officials of Longpo Gyakar Monastery, I gave the transmission for the *Eight Thousand Stanza*

Prajñaparamita Sutra and taught much dharma. I gave a number of empowerments in the context of a samaya substance and torma accomplishment assembly. Around one thousand five hundred people attended this. At Longpo Dechen Monastery, Lhalung, Tsikarley, and Lakha I performed dedications and affixed the seal of aspirations.

In every part of Nyangka Lungpa, including the three districts of Tu, Ding, and U, and the three of Ke, Nang, and Drak, I gave minor empowerments and authorizations. I made vast aspirations and dedications. An extremely large number of people attended these. At every village and monastery I visited I was welcomed with a reception, a ganachakra, music, and a procession. Amidst these ceremonies I revealed profound terma.

Invited to Sky Cave Snow Wall and Mön, I opened the door to a hidden sacred place and, based on a minor vision, revealed a few minor termas. I revealed others at Tsari Turquoise Lake and other sites such as Chartsa Monastery based on visions and on the appearance of a garuda.

The tulkus of Tsele Shika invited me there. I gave shramanera vows to about thirty aspiring monastics there, and offered much dharma including the empowerments of the *Very Profound Embodiment of the Three Jewels* and the *Heart Essence of Yutok*. At the Jowo of Kongpo I gave the empowerments and transmissions for *Liberation Through Hearing* to Ponlop Khyapdal Lhundrup, his nephew Karma Lhawang, and a crowd of about one thousand five hundred people. At Chöjung Monastery in Chimyül Tsagong I gave the transmission of the *Ultimate Point: Liberating All Beings*. In all the adjacent areas, such as Tsangpo Gokuk, I formed connections by giving empowerment and dharma. I cast grain on all the villagers, caused the blessings to descend into everyone within sight, and cultivated compassion for every living being I saw. I dedicated all of my practice, both elaborate and simple, to their awakening. Especially, I made vast aspirations for the benefit of every place I went or stayed. I dedicated feast offerings, offered white tormas, and offered my own aggregates as a feast.

Ever since I began to disseminate my newly revealed termas, for the last twelve years starting with the Bird Year, all fighting in this entire region has ceased. The harvests have been good; rainfall has been plentiful. Everyone around here feels happy and cheerful. Guru, three jewels, hear me! Look upon us with compassion!

I received many prophecies from dakinis regarding Bangri. Later Dakpo Norbu Gyenpa granted his assurance, so I came here free from doubt. I offered cleansing smoke and tormas to the resident gods, and thought, "While I have acquired the freedom and resources of a human body this once, up to now I have let my life go to waste; I must devote myself solely to practice from now on! No matter what I think about, I see it all as impermanent. No matter how one thinks about it, if holy dharma is not practiced, everything else we do is nothing more than a perversion of diligence. Oh, how sad!" The overpowering intensity of my recollection of Guru Rinpoche led me to compose this song of praise to this place:

Lords of compassion, three jewels,
Unfailing refuge, lord of dharma,
Padmasambhava, gaze lovingly
On me and all beings of the three realms!

In my youth I studied the science of medicine.
As a young man I practiced in retreat
And studied dharma as earnestly as I could.
This was not fruitless, Padmasambhava!

I've recited a hundred million mantras
And spent my days and nights in both
Elaborate and simple dharma practice.
I've revealed many very profound termas.
I'm no charlatan, Padmasambhava!

As I enter middle age all my doings
Are unlikely to be completely successful,
But I will bring both joy and sorrow to the path.
Father, let your blessings not be meager,
Padmasambhava!

An old man about to die, I will discard elaboration
And live in this place prophesied by the victors,
This Bangri Tashi Öbar.
Grant your blessing quickly, Padmasambhava!

All my past deeds have been like bubbles in water.
My future actions will be like dew on grass.
All of these are impermanent, like last night's dreams.
I think of this frequently, Padmasambhava!

Not deities with faces, hands, and jewelry,
Nor painted or sculpted:
I want to see the single natural deity!
Show me my own primordially pure mind,
Padmasambhava!

Not mantras of complex sound requiring careful
elocution,
But spontaneous, primordial vajra repetition:
I want to hear what is beyond vocalization!
Utter natural sound, Padmasambhava!

Not certain belief in a mind that is lasting or ending,
Something or nothing, to be gained or lost;
But natural, ordinary awareness:
Show me what cannot be shown, Padmasambhava!

Not the flowers offered to deities;
Nor the outer, inner, and secret offerings we solidify;
Not accumulation with fixation:
Complete my accumulations without gathering,
Padmasambhava!

Whatever remains of my short human life
I will spend in retreat and not waste.

Whether obstacles arise or siddhi,
I've no other refuge than you, Padmasambhava!

The greatest of your emanations,
Lord Buddha appearing as a human being,
Father Norbu Gyenpa, said this:
"Bangri Tashi Öbar is a beautiful, colorful
mountain
With excellent blessing and rocks like
Chinese drums and white conch shells.
Find that place and live there!"

Although there was no water this winter,
Once the ice melted a spring burst forth.
Many gates to sacred sites opened.
I've revealed many profound dharma termas here.

There are many wonders of which I could speak,
But if I did so now people wouldn't believe me.
The truth of what I say will become clear in time.

Guru Rinpoche placed his eight-petaled lotus feet
on this ground.
His throne and imprints of his head are still visible
here.
The virtues of this place are too many to list.
It is made of various precious stones.
It is the abode of the deities of secret mantra.

There is a conch Avalokiteshvara
Twenty-one male fathoms in height.

There is a turquoise Tara
Eighteen female fathoms high.
There are images of the eight lamps of this kalpa.
There are eight treasure vases.
There are many crystal cells.
There is a visible Vajravarahi of ruby.
This place is bursting with gold and silver.
It is bursting with the water of life.

Anyone with karma:
Have faith and respect for this place.
What help is there for people without karmic
connections?

I wrote many such songs; they can be found in my *Inner Memoir*.

At the time I thought, "It would be better for me to continue to practice in retreat than to accumulate stuff through a premature attempt to help other beings. Premature attempts to help beings are untrustworthy; I would be much happier devoting my life to retreat among the rocks and snows."

Although my thoughts were sincere and openly expressed, I already had a community of around forty people who depended on me as their teacher. My first monk was Padma Tendzin; he and I will remain together throughout both this and all future lives.

Because dwellings were scarce, we all worked hard on constructing little huts of earth and stone. Since then I have given the series of empowerments for the *Ocean of*

Sadhanas; the transmissions of the *Vajramala*, the *Thirty-Four Jatakas*, the *Hundred Jatakas*, the complete *Collected Works of King Songtsen Gampo*, the *Testament of Padma*, the *Golden Garland of the Kagyu*, and the writings of Milarepa, Trungpa Chözang Nyima, and Jetsun Lhatse Rinpoche; and many profound instructions of the Dakpo Kagyu including mahamudra, the six dharmas of Naropa, and identical flavor.

I have also given the transmissions of the Seventeen Tantras of the very secret upadesha class of the great perfection, the *Immaculate Confession Tantra*, and the *Life of Guru Chöwang*. I have given the great empowerment of Karma Lingpa's *Peaceful and Wrathful: Self-Liberated Wisdom*, a torma empowerment of the eight dispensations, and a symbolic empowerment using piles of grain. I have given the empowerments and transmissions of *Mahakarunika: Liberating All Beings*, a profound terma of the vidyadhara Vulture Feather; and those of the peaceful and wrathful Guru Rinpoche.

At the request of tantrikas I have given the empowerments and transmissions of the four-armed terma protector and of Kingkang Yamantaka, the three powerful deities of Yamantaka Ayupati, and Yamantaka Nagaraksha. I have given them the transmissions for protection, reversal, killing, control, burning, casting, dance ritual, mandala creation, melody, entrustment, piercing, binding, the yogic dances of celebration, songs of experience, torma rituals, effigy-substitution ransom rituals, and astrological calculation.

At the request of physicians I have given the transmissions of the *Four Medicinal Tantras*, their eighteen supplements, and the biographies of Yutok and Zungkar. I have given them the authorization and entrustment of Baishajyaguru and the empowerments and transmissions of the *Heart Essence of Yutok*, and taught them a great deal about medicine and dharma.

I have enabled every monk new to dharma to become a shramanera. To lay people I have taught the benefits of recitation of the six syllables and of the sutra and dharani of Amitayus, and have gotten them to take at least one vow. In particular I have taught women the benefits of taking refuge and the observance of fasting. Whenever a crowd has gathered, whether large or small, I have gotten them all to promise to perform life-release. I have encouraged children to become literate, have given whatever I could to beggars and dogs, and have dedicated cleansing smoke, singed offerings, and tormas to nonhumans. I have given out all the samaya substances and liberation-through-wearing yantras I could.

In sum, starting with the pratimoksha and single-day vows and all the way up to ati, the all-pervasive great perfection, I have tried to teach every aspect of dharma to the best of my knowledge. Really, once you recognize ordinary awareness, your primordially pure mind itself, knowing and not knowing no longer exist; they are merely the mind's complexion.

I have continually taught the *Very Profound Embodiment of the Three Jewels* and the *Secret Path*

Guruyoga of Gampopa; many people have practiced those sadhanas, and all of them have exhibited excellent signs without obstacle. A continuous stream of people, some learning to read and write, some requiring explanation of various words, some performing prostrations, some reciting mantra, some wanting to learn the meditation posture, some seeking to foster tranquility, some wishing to learn liturgical practices – all of them exerting themselves in good, virtuous practice – have appeared over the years; I think that this is due to the blessings of my guru and the three jewels.

Many have given me generous offerings, such as hundredfold offerings, gold, silver, copper, or iron. Some have given less, such as horses, dzos, yaks, coral, amber, turquoise, sapphire, cattle, grain, butter, tea, or silk. Some have given little, just scarves. Whether given a lot or a little, I have not allowed anything offered to me to go to waste. It has all been used to sponsor images of body, speech, and mind; feast offerings and other ritual materials; and the sangha.

When I lived at Sheltö I received all the instructions in detail, and tried to receive as many empowerments and transmissions as possible. I had studied medicine in order to make a living, and all the dharma I received in those days came from long lineages and involved many shastras. I have always wanted to rely on the profound termas of Guru Rinpoche. Their lineage is short. They are unpolluted by broken samaya or demonic possession and unmixed with the thinking of ordinary beings and dharma of Tibetan invention. They are the genuine, pure words of Guru Padma. I have always wanted to intensively practice the union of generation and completion, relying on a yidam like the red Wrathful Guru. My wishes have been accomplished.

All of my masters, teachers, and preceptors, as well as my parents, have repeatedly made the good aspiration that I be of great help to beings; this has helped me more than anything else. In spite of their great support, however, I have always had a hard time having faith in anyone; this is a grave flaw in my character.

To the monks gathered here at Bangri Tashi Öbar I have repeatedly said this:

"You are all here because you have faith in me; this is a result of good karmic residue. None of us is headed anywhere other than death; we therefore must exert ourselves in the practice of holy dharma. However, if we compare our lives to those of past victors, we seem to lack diligence.

"Learning to read and write is indispensable, as literacy is the foundation of holy dharma. The vows of either an upasaka or shramanera are also indispensable. Even if you are incapable of vast studies, the following liturgies are definitely necessary: the *Five Royal Sutras*, the *Seven Chapters*, the *Praise of Gampopa*, the short *Embodiment of the Three Jewels*, the Drukpa *Supplication for the Four Sessions*, and dedications and aspirations for all the teachings. If incapable of even that, exert yourself in the practice of the six syllables, prostrations, and tranquility meditation.

"The robes of a bhikshu or shramanera are definitely necessary, but if you cannot acquire them, no matter what you wear you must still behave in accordance with the rules of the vinaya; it is unfitting to just wear whatever is most comfortable or flattering.

"As liquor is the root of all evil, you must give it up. You must also seek at least part of your own supplies of food; I will supplement those with whatever meager food is offered to me. You need to be able to survive on a single meal each day consisting of tea, soup, and vegetables and live in little huts just big enough to contain you, made from stones and clay, remaining in retreat and silence. Living with others and a lot of conversation are contradictory to holy dharma. Also, entering villages inhabited by laypeople is contradictory to holy dharma. Even looking at them and having slight contact with them will ruin you.

"Donations made to the sangha are a major cause of obscuration. Eating meat specifically killed for your consumption is unbearably sad. If you seek material donations you will be able to get them anywhere, but you will have turned your back on holy dharma. Whether you think about the day or the night, if we don't achieve an undistracted mindfulness that mixes day and night we will only end up in one of samsara's six states.

"I am not going to travel. If you can put up with austerity and meager food, I will teach you whatever dharma I know. If you can spend your lives on this mountain with just enough shelter and clothing so you don't freeze to death and just enough food so you don't starve to death, and avoid being burned by donations to the sangha, the compassion of the three jewels will manifest.

"If you can't live like that and are hoping that I will feed and clothe you, please go elsewhere as soon as possible. Whatever resources I have are not at the disposal of those who seek to practice dharma in comfort; if they were, it would be wrong and a disgrace in the sight of the three jewels. There is no point in our doing things that will only cause the ruination of ourselves and others.

"We must be diligent in meditation in mountain retreats among the rocks. Guru Rinpoche has said that many people will become vidyadharas, siddhas, by practicing the profound dharma he has given me. Don't forget these words of mine; dissolve them into your hearts."

These are my memoirs in brief from the time of my birth from my mother up to my forty-first year. They are without hypocrisy or concealment. I have not lied, claiming to be or have anything I am not or have not. I have hidden nothing, whether good or bad; those with eyes of wisdom see this. May the goodness and merit of this lead the minds of all beings of the three realms to holy dharma! May they be ripened, liberated, and achieve great awakening!

Chapter Two: 1627–1635

I, the great vidyadhara, wrote this long poem of concern at a time when my community was in turmoil:

NAMO GURU PADMA SIDDHI HUM HRIH
Now adversity and obstacles have great force.
Evil maras are active.
Beings, poisoned, have little merit.

The elements in my body are askew.
All this impermanence makes me sad.
If I must leave this world for the next
I've no regrets but a few concerns.

The great prophecies of Guru Rinpoche
Are only half fulfilled; this concerns me.
The time to disclose profound termas
I've revealed has not come,

So I must reconceal them; this concerns me.

I have not yet passed the whispered lineage of
profound dharma
To some of the fortunate who are devoted to me;
this concerns me.
I have not yet shown some close, trusted friends
That Buddha is in the palm of their hands;
this concerns me.

I have helpful, practical instructions to give
That disciples have not yet requested;
this concerns me.
I have the power to eradicate harmful enemies and
obstructors
But few have asked for guidance in how to do so;
this concerns me.

I have a lot of profound dharma suitable to tame
different people
But few possess intelligent, clear minds;
this concerns me.

I've opened the door to a treasury of empowerment,
transmission, and instruction
But people with past training are rare;
this concerns me.

There must be many people with karmic connections
to me
But many of those haven't met me; this concerns me.

The great perfection can liberate just through being heard,
But what about our lineage of the vinaya? This concerns me.

All I think about is these monks of mine,
But they're still young; this concerns me.
They all want to study and practice,
But they have endless work to do; this concerns me.

I intend to teach profound dharma to all devoted to me,
But what if I die now? This concerns me.

Shakyamuni, Padmasambhava, Gampopa, Lord Mipam:
Avert untimely death, three jewels!
Remove adversity and obstacles, Avalokita!
May my wishes be accomplished according to dharma, Singhamukha!

The Bangri tertön wrote this thinking of impermanence and death
On the tenth day of the tenth month in the Year of the Horse,
While his community was in turmoil.
Those with faith and devotion, keep it in mind!
By this virtue may all beings achieve omniscient buddhahood.

I was then repeatedly invited to Powo Yegong by Tsering

Gyalmo, so I set off in that direction. By way of the Tawa Demo Pass and Lolam Nakpo I traveled to Pepetang, Dokar Monastery, Menchu Monastery, Zurdong, and Senge Dzong. In particular I stayed for about a month and a half in the lower valley of Makulungpa, where I performed an empowerment-accomplishment of the *Embodiment of the Three Jewels* and deciphered the profound dharma *Mahakarunika: The Self-Liberation of Lower States*. Tremendous benefit for beings through holy dharma occurred there. I offered Pönlop Ugyen Tendzin and Bhaka Tulku many empowerments and transmissions, and received much profound dharma from them in return. I also taught terma dharma to many major and minor lamas of the area. The local communities offered me their own earth and sky as well as actual material offerings of horses, dzos, brocade, silk, cotton, and silver; the value of these offerings came to around five hundred loads of tea. I sealed all of these with dedication and aspirations, sponsored communal tea service in most of the monasteries throughout Kongpo, sent offerings to all of the lamas with whom I'd formed a dharma connection, gave gifts to all my monks, disciples, and donors, and expanded the retreat facility at Bangri.

Not long after that I went to central Tibet. At Tölung Tsurphu I met the Gyalwang Karmapa Chöying Dorje and offered him all my dharma of profound terma as well as the many wonderful terma items I had recovered thus far, greatly pleasing him. I also offered him thirty silver scarves, thirteen measures of gold, a hundred and eight measures of silver, eleven horses and mules, several loads of tea, silk, cotton, and butter – all told, a hundredfold offering. I also presented offerings to his great disciples, including Gyaltsap Rinpoche, Situ Rinpoche, and the Karmapa's secretary. I sponsored tea service at most of the monasteries of central Tibet, as well as prayer flags for the sake of auspiciousness.

The Gyalwang Karmapa bestowed upon me a brocade-bound letter bearing his seal, a set of the three robes, a cloak, a vajra and bell, a canopy, and other generous gifts. He proclaimed auspiciousness and was very loving and compassionate to me. Both he, the father, and his disciples, the sons, have been very supportive of me. I was later able to offer Gyaltsap Rinpoche in particular further empowerments, transmissions, instruction, and oral guidance according to the whispered lineage; his mind and mine became one. He also recognized me as a nirmanakaya of Nyangben Tingdzin Zangpo.

At that time the ruler of Tsang sent me an invitation to his kingdom by messenger. As my divination was not propitious, I sent back a message that I would visit at a later time. At Rechungpa's Cave I offered the empowerments and transmissions of my profound termas to the dharma lord Dzamling Yongdrak, and received from him the complete old and new *Whispered Lineage of Rechungpa*. At Drikung Dzongsar I received from Shapdrung Könchok Puntsok the collected works of his predecessor Namchak Mebar and the *Very*

Profound Intention. In return I offered him the empowerments and transmissions of my new termas and other profound Nyingma dharma; we established an excellent connection.

I stayed for more than a week at the Urusha Temple, sponsored by the eastern Tibetan Lama Padma Lodrö. Amidst a gathering of many major and minor lamas I again taught all of my new termas and gave their empowerments and authorizations. Entrusting the samaya-bound Vajrasadhu with their protection, I secretly revealed many termas there.

From Kundun Riwang, a seventh-generation descendant of the tertön Sangye Lingpa, I received the profound dharma of the *Wisdom Assembly of the Guru* and the biographies of the tertön and his sons. In return I offered Kundun Riwang many empowerments and much dharma.

From a great perfection lama from Latö, I received the *Five Testaments* and Dungtso Repa's *Black Yangti*. In return I offered him many empowerments and much dharma, especially those of my new termas. At that time I also received a letter and a prayer for my longevity from Lhatse Tulku Rinpoche.

I offered empowerments, transmissions, and instructions to Nedong Gongma Rinpoche, the king of a wooded area of southern Tibet. I was invited to officiate at the funeral of the Shapdrung of Tsongdü Draka. This was attended by more than a thousand monks, whom I led in the making of dedications and aspirations; I received extensive hundredfold offerings. Also, a new edition of the *Translated Words of the Buddha* had just been printed there, so I consecrated it properly at Öngyalzang, brought needed rainfall, and gave empowerments and dharma to all present. From Janak Dordzin Gongma Rinpoche I received the *Razor Trilogy*. In turn I offered him a great many empowerments and teachings of the new and ancient traditions.

In sum, I established profound dharma connections with all the monastics and laypeople in the south, including the areas of Jar, Nyal, and Loro. I gave empowerments, transmissions, and instructions in profound dharma to the dharma king Jarpa Tripön, his queen, and his children. I also convened a great accomplishment assembly and amrita consecration at his court. In all I've traveled throughout these southern areas three times. In particular, because of my strong past karmic connection with Shapdrung Rinpoche, he opened the door to my helping beings in that region. He has real faith in me; because his mind and mine have mixed, I have offered him extraordinary terma items and always keep him in mind.

I was welcomed to the Pekar College of Jampa Chöling by a procession including parasols, victory banners, music, and other offerings. I gave the sangha there the transmission of the *Testament of Padma* and many empowerments and transmissions from my new termas. I offered the transmission and instructions of the great perfection to Pekar Rinpoche and the rebirth of the dharma lord vidyadhara.

The omniscient Gyalwang Drukpa was in strict retreat at Sangak Chöling; I met with him in his retreat house and offered him the *Svabhavikakaya Gurusadhana* and other teachings.

I was invited to Sumkar Nödzey Castle in Kongpo by Achey Wangmo, Shalngo Salney, and Abo Lhawang Namgyal; I convened an accomplishment assembly of the new terma *Mahakarunika: Self-Liberation of Lower States* there. An extremely large number of people attended it.

At the time an obstructive ailment had spread in the area, causing the deaths of many people. I performed a public Parnashavari authorization, dedicated white tormas to local spirits, and invoked the power of truth; the sickness ended.

That year, starting from Bangri Tashi Öbar, I journeyed through the central mountains and visited famous places such as Lhasa, Samye, Chimpu, Tradruk, Gungtang, Yerpa, Umbu Lakar, the Stone Temple of Önjang, Zangyak Rock, Tromo Rock, Kyungtsang Rock, Zemo Mountain, Tsetang Gönpo Mountain, the Crystal Cave of Yarlung, Daklha Gampo, Pamodru, Densatil, Tölung Tsurphu, Drikung Tel, Rechungpa's Cave, Jowo Boka, Tsari, Tsakong, Tsanang, Mön, Tselagang, Drakarlha Tsering, and Kongpo Gyala.

While staying in these sacred places I witnessed an inconceivably great variety of signs in actuality, hypnagogia, and dreams; I will not write of these in detail for fear of excessive prolixity.

I offered empowerments, transmissions, instructions, and guidance to many major and minor lamas and masters; and received much dharma in return. If I set forth a rough list of those to whom I've offered profound dharma, they are led by my root guru, my holy source of refuge, Mipam Tashi Lodrö; the crown jewel of this Himalayan land, the Gyalwang Karmapa Chöying Dorje, father and sons; Norbu Gyenpa, the supreme nirmanakaya of Daklha Gampo, as well as his disciples; the omniscient Gyalwang Drukpa Paksam Wangpo, father and sons; the dharma lord of Drikung, Könchok Puntsok, along with his retinue; Chögowa, father and sons; the great khenpo of Maldro Katsal Tel; the khenpo of Yangpachen; the dharma lord of Rechungpa's Cave; the lama of Chongyal Palri with his disciples; the lamas of Yarlung Sheldrak; the nirmanakaya of Samye; Gongkar Shapdrung; the Drakar Shapdrung of Lhagyal Riwa; the Jarpa Tripön; the lamas of Chögyal Podrang, Tashi Tse, Namse Ling, and Nyingpu and Jachung in Kongpo; Chöjung Lama; Tsele Tulku Natsok Rangdröl; the lama of Tsangpo Gokuk; the lamas of Dechen Monastery; Lopön Damchö Puntsok; the dharma lord Gyalwang Kukye; the dharma lord of Pende; Powo Bhakha Tulku; Pönlop Ugyen Tendzin; the lama of Pepetang; the lama of Tawa Tsigeteng; the lama of Menmo; the lama of Deyangtsonang; and many other major and minor lamas in Nyangka.

My connection with all of these great lamas and great personages has seemed to arise as a result of my merit, for they are all great beings with whom any connection is beneficial; they are also all individuals prophesied by Guru Rinpoche.

I have never wasted anything I have been given by those worthy beings with karmic destiny, by male or female donors, or by devoted monks or other disciples – even as little as a cup of flour; I have sealed every offering with dedication and aspiration, increasing its merit until it filled all space.

The number of men and women, both monastics and laypeople, whose hair I've cut must exceed three hundred. Many holy beings have come here to Bangri. The disciples accompanying me on my travels have numbered more than eighty. Usually there are about seventy sangha members living here at Bangri when I'm here; the number of people I have to feed here has never been less than thirty. On tenth days and other special occasions I serve tea and feasts to all who come. There is an unending stream of people who come here to request empowerments, transmissions, and instruction – at least one or two arrive every day. Several people have entered yearlong retreats here.

Briefly put, I have given something to every monastic or layperson who has ever come here: medicine, edible yantras, protection from poison or disease, blessing through touch, and/or samaya pills. I have never turned anyone away; no one has left here empty-handed. Before every teaching session I have recited the seven branches, lit incense, set out whatever offerings I could, recited the six syllables, and served tea to everyone attending the teaching. I have evenly distributed any and all extra clothing given to me. I have even helped many beings through the distribution of my urine. I have helped beings in every way I could, even by scolding and hitting them when necessary. I've brought some to holy dharma by acting the way they do. Although beings in these final days are hard to tame, I've tried to skillfully and kindly help them in every direct or indirect way possible.

Even when I eat my single daily meal, I always first recite the *Sutra of the Recollection of the Noble Three Jewels*, and conclude the meal with a single recitation of the Heart Sutra. It makes no difference to me whether I recite them or not; I do it to serve as a good example. I think we need to constantly remain in the posture and gaze of meditation and make sure that everything that comes out of our mouths accords with holy dharma; I am always mindful of this. Never being without the three robes serves to inspire beings. I also drink no more than three cups of tea daily. I hope that all of this makes me a good example. My constant, sincere, and honest prayer is this:

Guru and the three jewels,
May my body, speech, and mind benefit all beings
throughout space.
May my every action lead to great good for beings.
May I never give rise for even an instant to a
thought other than holy dharma.
If I ever do, may it not be accomplished.

> May I perfect all of the intentions of all Buddhas of the three times!

I make this aspiration constantly, without allowing my mouth to rest.

In order to really help beings, a sincerely pure motivation based on love and compassion is extremely important. In particular, although the four ways of attracting beings are taught, I've never been able to engage in them. Nevertheless, I really do whatever is best for beings, right now and into the distant future.

The presence of precious images of body, speech, and mind, and of the sangha, in an otherwise uninhabited wilderness is a sign that the Buddha's teachings are flourishing.

No matter where I go, everyone treats me with so much veneration that the very earth and stones hum with it; this is due to the kindness of the three jewels. No matter where I stay, I am surrounded by people learning to read and write, studying terminology, performing liturgies and rituals of fulfillment and reconciliation, and playing liturgical music so that the very air hums with low notes, shakes with high notes, and sings and throbs with percussion; this is a sign that the Buddha's teachings are flourishing.

The roar of the conch shell summoning monks to tea and assembly and the long lines of maroon and gold as the sangha gathers are evidence of service to the teachings.

The melodious chanting of prayers throughout the

four sessions, the piercing call of thighbone trumpets, the explosive thunder of PHAT, and the sweet melody of the seven branches are decorative evidence of the existence of a practice community.

Square huts barely big enough for one person, painted bright white and flying fluttering prayer flags, are signs of the existence of a retreat.

The ringing sound of small cymbals and the sweet ring of bells are signs of the existence of a practice community.

The beat of drums and tinkle of cymbals, the laughing call of thighbone trumpets, and the waving of banners of beckoning are signs of the approach of protectors.

The donning of brilliant costumes; the graceful performance of dance and melody; the casting of tormas as magical weapons accompanied by the incitement of forceful mantras; and the activities of fire offering, control, and liberation are signs that the dharma of tantrikas has not disappeared.

Thrones, canopies, parasols, victory banners, cloaks, lotus crowns with vulture feathers, mandalas, and empowerment implements are both pleasing to the three jewels and inspiring to those with faith.

The teaching of dharma, the giving of empowerments, the melodious chanting of mantras, and the descent of blessings open the door to helping beings.

The offerings and service presented by those with faith; the adornment of master and disciples by dharma robes, skirts, and hats; the melodious song of liturgy, and the harmonious proclamation of auspiciousness are ways for those with faith to accumulate merit.

The fact that when adherents of other traditions eloquently expound their positions I am not timid or tongue-tied, but am able to explain our position as clearly and concisely as a flash of lightning and based on the Buddha's words is a sign that the teachings of monastic colleges are flourishing.

The ceaseless stream of people seeking profound instruction, performing prostrations or circumambulation, or entirely focused on correct meditation posture and gaze is a sign that meditation instruction based on the inner meaning is flourishing.

The presence of some who expel their stale breath with a whoosh, hold vase breaths, practice yogic exercises with resounding smacks, and practice the ejection of consciousness is a sign that dharma of the definitive meaning is flourishing.

The people who come from everywhere merely to be blessed by the touch of my hand, just because they have heard my name, do so because of their aspirations in past lives.

Some people with impure perception denigrate me. Unaware of their own failure to even acquire food and clothing and their own desperation, they devote themselves to gossip. Although there are such people, I have studied assiduously, kept my samaya and vows purely, practiced enough that I am unashamed, exhibited signs of attainment, and helped beings. To those who denigrate me I say, "Just try to do no worse than me; you will not disgrace the Buddha's teachings!" Ha, ha!

It is said that the happiness of beings depends on the Buddha's teachings, that the Buddha's teachings depend on the sangha, and that the sangha depends on its aspirations to both study and practice. It is also said that good tantrikas are the fence that protects the teachings. Is there then any error in my ways? Think carefully, all you with experience of dharma.

Some Drukpa yogis, unaware that they are simultaneously experiencing both the cause and result of being pretas, their bodies without vows, their speech without liturgy, their minds without dharma, their hands without possessions, who cover mountainsides with their shit, turn over in their beds and return to sleep at dawn, and stretch out for more rest at sunrise say, "The termas supposedly revealed by the tertön of Bangri were written by Shapdrung Norbu Gyenpa of Daklha Gampo; they are fake. The so-called 'tertön' merely pretends to have revealed them as terma."

If this were true, all of the greatest lamas of Tibet and many minor ones would be my dupes. However, my opponents' words would seem to be incorrect.

The yogis of Sheltö appear to have taken against me as soon as they first heard my name. It seems more appropriate for me to simply say "Yuck!" than to exclaim "Oh! How sad!"

Were I not concerned with possible contravention of my samaya with the precious dharma lord Mipam Tashi

Lodrö I would not even consider those Mara-possessed, samaya-breaking, evil beggars to be human. Their very existence is a bad sign. I have come to regard them as a disgrace to the Buddha's teachings.

Even here at Bangri, I have become displeased by a few monks who've taken to drink. If holy dharma does not occur, there is no point in having many monks. Although I support them with food, clothing, and dharma they are ungrateful. They don't listen to the dharma I teach, but are diving head first into the swamp of samsara. When I see such people I am saddened.

No matter to whom I give them, my possessions and resources, having been offered to me, are like virulent poison when consumed by anyone else. On the other hand, those who wander off to distant places become so desperate that they are forced to take the lives of animals, eat their flesh, and drink their blood; this touches my heart. Very few end up living virtuously.

The need to please male and female donors makes me angry. When I think about the lives of victors of the past, our current custom of traveling throughout the land and saying of it, "I have benefited beings," is horrifying. Many lamas drink beer, eat food offered to them in faith, and live amongst flocks of women. Oh, they even end up killing the babies born by their female "disciples" in order to conceal their birth. It would be better to be an ordinary layperson than such a lama!

I don't know how long I'm going to stay in this world. If I could spend the rest of my life amongst beautiful mountains and pure water with about four or five disciples, dwelling in simple retreat huts, trying our best to live in accord with holy dharma, I would be content and my practice would progress. If I could live on an isolated mountainside lightly forested by juniper, with plentiful sunshine and fine fragrance, a clean and pleasant environment conducive to both health and clarity, with sweet birdcalls and particularly the "Ko! Ko!" of ptarmigans, where animals play and run about, where one can see majestic rocky peaks and grassy hills, a cheerful place where one is serenaded by the sound of rushing water and soothed by the wafting scent of juniper, spending the rest of my life in retreat in a mud hut, how happy I would be! I think of this frequently.

Looking at it another way, however, my desire to be alone could be a sign that I'm straying on to the path of a shravaka or pratyekabuddha, or even a sign of impending death. According to Guru Rinpoche's prophecies regarding my benefit of beings, until four destined disciples born through their aspirations have gathered around me my individual service to beings will only be mediocre. Those four disciples have not yet appeared.

Without a dharma community, if I had to train disciples by wandering through village after village I think I would have a very hard time. The monasteries around here are not very helpful. The people who gather around me don't think about dharma; most of them only think about food and clothing.

Those monks who like beer do not agree with my

disposition; I am concerned that over time this might lead to a great herd of people with broken samaya. Please, everyone, keep that in mind!

Around the time of which I was writing above I received the bad news that the mind of the nirmanakaya of Daklha Gampo had dissolved into the dharmadhatu. After hearing this, no matter what I thought of, I was depressed. Because of the paucity of beings' merit and good karma, within a span of two years the omniscient Shamar Chökyi Wangchuk, the lord Pawo Tsuklak Gyamtso, and the supreme nirmanakaya of Daklha Gampo had all passed away. Hearing this saddened me to a point of real unhappiness. Since I could think of no effective remedy for this loss, I became depressed.

At the time a lot of people came to me, asking for written advice. Unable to write individually to each of them, I wrote these instructions for all my followers:

OM MANI PADME HUM HRIH!
Buddha Shakyamuni, source of the teachings;
Guru Rinpoche, lotus-born body of light;
Songtsen Gampo, who made Tibet a happy place;
Peerless Gampopa, crown jewel of the practice lineage;
Karmapa, who helps beings again and again;
And Lord Mipam Tashi Lodrö, whose kindness is beyond repayment:
I prostrate to you, holy sources of refuge!

Bless me so that my benefit for beings may be inconceivably great.

Some of those who depend on me don't understand
Even though I've spread profound dharma all over.
They say "I need further verses of instruction."
If so, I offer these to the ears of all my followers.

Since the day I was born to my mother I have,
Because of good habits, gone for refuge to the three jewels.
I've always felt death and impermanence in my depths.
All my actions have been those of holy dharma.
These are the deeds of this old man.
Please, my followers, act as I have.

At the start I was unmistaken in finding an authentic guru.
In the middle I was unmistaken in gaining self-confidence through instruction.
In the end I was unmistaken in practice and achieved siddhi.
Now my assistance to beings is not small, but useful to all.
These are the deeds of this old man.
Please, my followers, act as I have.

Although I was born at the end of time when the lifespan's only forty,
I've tried my best at holy, divine dharma.

I've avoided wrongdoing to the best of my ability.
My behavior's not been coarse, but careful.
These are the deeds of this old man.
Please, my followers, act as I have.

Although I was born a child of common evildoers
I followed good examples and studied hard.
I entered the bodhisattva path by leaving home as
a youth.
Unstained by downfalls, I've learned to trust myself.
These are the deeds of this old man.
Please, my followers, act as I have.

Seeing that causality is infallible, I practiced hard.
For twenty-five years I abstained from meat,
Living on minerals and eating only once a day.
I've never been without the three robes of dharma.
These are the deeds of this old man.
Please, my followers, act as I have.

Seeing the consumption of offerings as poison,
In retreat I lived on three-day soup,
And everything I did was motivated by bodhichitta.
I worked hard, never straying into the pretty dharma
of convenience.
These are the deeds of this old man.
Please, my followers, act as I have.

I lived alone, at the cost of food, clothing,
and conversation.
If victors of the past saw me, they must have rejoiced.

I automatically repaid the kindness of my parents.
Sad, I practice diligently out of the desire to be free.
These are the deeds of this old man.
Please, my followers, act as I have.

I unreservedly dedicated all the virtue I've gathered
with my three gates
To beings of the three realms and six states, objects
of compassion,
And prayed for them. I've not strayed onto the paths
Of shravakas or pratyekabuddhas; I've entered the
mahayana.
These are the deeds of this old man.
Please, my followers, act as I have.

From the Year of the Male Earth Monkey to that
of the Female Wood Ox,[12]
For seventeen years, I raised the victory banner of
practice.
I didn't stray into sloth or laziness; I practiced
dharma.
"Experienced practitioners," think carefully!
These are the deeds of this old man.
Please, my followers, act as I have.

I never let my body rest; I prostrated and
circumambulated.
I never let me speech rest; I recited liturgy
and mantras.
I never let my mind wander; I stabilized mindfulness.

12. 1608–1625.

I was immersed in luminosity all day and night.
These are the deeds of this old man.
Please, my followers, act as I have.

I gained the warmth of chandali, my channels and winds trained.
I recited more than ten million yidam mantras.
I lived according to the vinaya and the ten dharma practices.
Think about all this, people who practice dharma!
These are the deeds of this old man.
Please, my followers, act as I have.

Because of past lives' karma, I encountered Padma's profound terma.
Clouds of dharma gathered around the slopes of Bangri.
Melodious thunder roared in every direction.
Amid lightning-flashes of signs of siddhi a great rain of instructions fell.
These are the deeds of this old man.
Please, my followers, act as I have.

When I was still young my fortitude
In holy dharma was not little.
Without regrets, I'm filled with joy.
Now that I'm old, my benefit of beings is not little.
These are the deeds of this old man.
Please, my followers, act as I have.

Through the power of the three jewels, those
embodiments of compassion,
Profound terma dharma fills all of Tibet.
I've offered it to all the great and minor lamas of
this snowy land.
My merit is not little; I am content.
These are the deeds of this old man.
Please, my followers, act as I have.

I don't know now if I'll stay in this world for long;
This makes me unhappy.
Who knows what past karma lies in wait?
But I'll have no regrets when I die, three jewels!
These are the deeds of this old man.
Please, my followers, act as I have.

When the momentum of this life wears out
I'm going to the pure realm of Chamaradvipa.[13]
I've ways to lead there all with good or bad
connections to me.
Those with faith, how fortunate you are!
These are the deeds of this old man.
Please, my followers, act as I have.

13. The pure realm of Guru Rinpoche.

My followers with faith and devotion,
Don't waste your lives! Live in retreat!
Living alone brings death and impermanence
to mind.
When sharp sadness arises, dharma has begun.

These are the deeds of this old man.
Please, my followers, act as I have.

In these days, the end of time,
We can't study much; look at your mind.
Repeat OM MANI PADME HUM, the essence of dharma.
Strip your mind down to naked lucidity-emptiness;
  that is profound.
These are the deeds of this old man.
Please, my followers, act as I have.

Why have you come to this retreat?
No one is your master; you're no one's servant.
You've no mundane work, and no holy dharma.
Don't fool yourselves; practice!
These are the deeds of this old man.
Please, my followers, act as I have.

As it is the root of evil, don't drink liquor.
As it is death for a practitioner, abstain from sex.
As they are an obstacle, be cautious in your use
  of donations.
Think carefully about your own life.
These are the deeds of this old man.
Please, my followers, act as I have.

Recite the refuge, bodhichitta, and hundred syllables
  in all four sessions.
Offer mandalas, pray, dedicate, and make aspirations.

Offer outer and inner tormas, daily confession, and other observances.
Above all else, repeatedly establish mindfulness.
These are the deeds of this old man.
Please, my followers, act as I have.

Outwardly, act so that you not cause gossip.
Inwardly, live in harmony with all your fellow monks.
Keep your samaya and vows purely and without destructive conflict.
Live like that and you will be both admired and happy.
These are the deeds of this old man.
Please, my followers, act as I have.

Lots of talk and lots of doings beckon disaster.
The pursuit of sex and liquor disgraces the three jewels.
If you contradict your guru's mind, you're a samaya-breaker.
Always be sensible, fortunate ones!
These are the deeds of this old man.
Please, my followers, act as I have.

One day Mara, Death, will come for you.
If you are not without regrets on that day
You will have made a fool of yourself.
Think about yourself starting right now.
These are the deeds of this old man.

Please, my followers, act as I have.

One day you will undergo the terrifying bardo.
Practice leapover and ejection now.
Unveil your mind and sustain the great perfection.
Work hard now; you'll need these instructions then.
These are the deeds of this old man.
Please, my followers, act as I have.

Whatever you do during the four types of activity,
It must be dharma including motivation, practice, and dedication.
The point of all this comes down to doing whatever
Your guru commands; there is nothing better than that.
These are the deeds of this old man.
Please, my followers, act as I have.

I'm unable to write separate instructions for each young monk,
But I've written this to all who have faith in me,
Male, female, lay, or monastic.
Keep all this in mind; it will help you.
These are the deeds of this old man.
Please, my followers, act as I have.

14. 1633.

I, the great vidyadhara of Bangri, wrote this
On the tenth day of the first month in the Year of the Bird[14]
As instructions for all my followers.
May this help all beings of the three realms!

Really, I've come to realize that if you have no cause to be ashamed of yourself; have entrusted yourself to your guru and the three jewels and offered them your body, speech, and mind; are never without love and compassion for all beings of the six states, who have all been our parents repeatedly throughout time without beginning; guard your samaya and vows as you do your eyes; do your best to act according to the vinaya so well taught by the Buddha; possess the pure perception of your three gates as the three mandalas, the brilliant radiance of your unaltered, relaxed mind; and are immersed in the good path of the ten dharma practices, this is the true way to achieve buddhahood.[15]

15. The ten dharma practices are copying the Buddha's words, making offerings, giving to those in need, listening to dharma, memorizing it, reading it, teaching it, reciting it, thinking about it, and meditating on it.

As for me, my practice schedule from dawn to midnight is this: At dawn, as soon as I awake, I recite the *Hundredfold Multiplication of Virtuous Deeds*, the blessing of speech, and the dharani of the Sanskrit vowels and consonants. Then, imagining my root guru above my head surrounded by the sources of refuge, I take refuge and generate bodhichitta wholeheartedly. I then recite the seven branches, the *Confession of Downfalls*, and the *Prostrations and Offerings to the Pratimoksha Lineage*; and receive renewal and purification.

I then recite the dharani of Vajravidarana three times and imagine a circle of protection, more or less elaborate depending on circumstances. I then recite the hundred syllables; offer outer, inner, and secret mandalas; practice guru yoga; and receive the four empowerments.

Then I recite a number of blessed liturgies, including

Increasing the Virtuous Power of Liturgy and Mantra, the *Self-Liberation of Habits*, and the long dharani of *Liberation Through Wearing*.

I then recite a thousand of each of these essence mantras: Guru Vajradhara, father and mother; the seven-syllable mantra of Chakrasamvara; Vajravarahi with the two faces of truth; and Amitayus. In particular I repeat the dharani of longevity a number of times equal to my years. I conclude this first session with my best effort at pacification.

At sunrise I offer a hundred prostrations and a hundred water tormas and recite the *Five Royal Sutras*, the *Aspiration of Maitreya*, both *White* and *Green Tara*, the *Confession of the Fourteen Root Downfalls*, the *Aspiration to Excellent Conduct*, the *Recitation of Mañjushri's Names*, the *Praise of the Buddha's Twelve Deeds*, the *Praise of Gampopa*, and other liturgies. Principally, I repeat a thousand MANIs, a hundred of the *Heart Sutra* mantra, and many other dharanis and mantras of Buddhas and bodhisattvas. I conclude the second session with the action of enrichment, including meditation on wealth deities.

During the afternoon session I repeat the hundred syllables a hundred times, the mantra of Hayagriva a thousand times, and perform both fulfillment and supplication of dharmapalas along with a feast offering. I engage in actions of power, including meditation on both the red Wrathful Guru and Dorje Trolö.

At dusk I offer my aggregates as a feast, recite the

Seven Chapters, repeat the combined mantra of the Eight Dispensations a thousand times, and recite the sadhanas of the following deities: the Peaceful and Wrathful Deities, the Eight Dispensations, Yamantaka Ayupatikala, Yamantaka Nagaraksha, Vajrabhairava, the Three Fierce Deities, various forms of Vajrapani derived from the oral and terma teachings, the dakini Singhamukha, the glorious Intersex Mahakala with his two brothers, the Four-Armed Mahakala, the Six-Armed Mahakala, Mahakali Vetali, Tseringma with her four sisters, Kongtsun Demo, Rahula, and Vajrasadhu. I also practice various secret sadhanas in that fourth session as well as the action of force.

In each of those four sessions I take refuge and generate bodhichitta, either extensively or concisely, and offer the seven branches. Between sessions I give empowerments, teach, write, and sometimes study the lives and writings of past victors. I also sometimes prepare herbal medicine, or prepare samaya substances and edible yantras.

Really, no matter how long the day and how short the night, while I devote more time to them at some times than at others, I have never omitted any of my elaborate yidam practices. Among these yidams, the main ones are Chakrasamvara, Amitabha, Avalokita, the peaceful and wrathful forms of Guru Rinpoche, Hayagriva, Vajrapani, Vajravarahi, and Singhamukha. I continue to practice them all so that I never waste my three gates and continue to help beings. I have never dwelt in mindless delusion devoid of freedom. Through mindfulness, I have never done anything that contravened dharma. All you who have clamored for my memoirs, keep that in your hearts!

It is my aspiration that, through unmistaken interdependence and intentions, my behavior become all the more disciplined and accord all the more with the vinaya as I age. Through the instructions on love and compassion, may my benefit for beings increase. May I never stray from my past engagement in the ten dharma practices. May I continuously become more and more diligent in my performance of elaborate practices. May I give ever more to beings, both dharma and material things. May my hermitage be ever more isolated, ever higher on the mountainside, as I age. In short, my prayer is that, as I age, I be ever more enthusiastic in every action that accords with dharma. All you who've said you wanted my memoirs, keep this in your hearts!

These are the brief memoirs of the vidyadhara Jatsön Nyingpo up to the age of fifty. I wrote all this myself; it has not been added to by others. There is also a large volume containing my writings on how to reach sacred sites, spontaneous instructions, and various legends; however, as I regard these as nothing more than my having set down whatever occurred to me at the time, I see no great value in them.

I wrote this in prompt response to the request of fortunate disciples.
If you don't take advantage of a momentary recollection,
You may never remember it again; so I hurried.
It's not all based on distant memories, though; I had some notes from the past.
Aside from that there's no end to what I could say or write,
But there's little point in writing it all down.
I've not included mundane stories, legends, or demagoguery.
I've not used too much vernacular or excessively frank language.
This is unobscured by the black rain-clouds of my shoddy poetry.
I've written benevolently in relaxed, unaltered mind-itself.
By the virtue of this may all beings throughout space achieve buddhahood.
MANGALAM!

Chapter Three: 1636–1639

GURU PADMA SIDDHI HUM HRIH!

Then, in my fifty-first year, I convened an amrita accomplishment assembly at the great temple of Nyalrong Podrang Yangtse. The Shapdrung, his consort, his entire entourage, sanghas of both the Sarma and Nyingma traditions, and three descendants of Guru Chöwang from Lhodrak along with some of their disciples all joined me.

For all of them, as well as a large gathering of tantrikas and monastics from the region, I let fall a rain of dharma including the empowerments, transmissions, and profound instructions of termas both old and new over the course of one month and eighteen days.

When I performed a public empowerment for around five thousand people the Shapdrung and his consort presented elaborate hundredfold offerings. Jarpa Tripön himself stood up and cast many measures of gold toward my face, amazing the entire crowd.

I also performed public empowerments and taught at Jar Taktse and Nemo. I then founded a college for the study and practice of my new termas at Jar Sungnyen Monastery. The Tripön and his consort supplied all the needed resources and supplies, including food allowances and the creation of the facility itself, for one hundred and thirteen monastics. I also gave them whatever support I could, but later on Pehar brought them a major obstacle; there was nothing to be done.

I then went to Dakpo Tsele by way of Karpo Pass. They welcomed me with a procession, and demonstrated tremendous pleasure at my arrival. I gave all of the empowerments and transmissions from my new termas, from the earliest up to the most recent, to the sangha there, which was headed by the nirmanakaya of Shapdrung Tutop Namgyal.

Next I went to Daklha Gampo, where I cast five measures of gold at the silver stupa enshrining the remains of Shapdrung Norbu Gyenpa. I wept copiously while doing this. I also offered much dharma, whatever they wanted, to the two descendants of Gampopa's family.

Continuing my journey, I met with the precious dharma lord Mipam Tashi Lodrö, whom I offered several things, such as a fine steed and a copper frying pan. I also offered him my most recent termas, such as the transmission for the first half of the *Glorious Intersex Protector*

Cycle and the authorization for the *Dorje Trolö Cycle*. Our minds were united.

Returning to Bangri Tashi Öbar, I entered retreat. I offered a little to the local people, and made offerings to all the major and minor lamas at all the larger and smaller monasteries in the area with the thought that it would be good to request their dedications at the time of my death in advance of that event.

To all my new and old monks and disciples, my close and distant male and female donors, and all my friends, I gave appropriate gifts, such as fabric and protection knots. I offered herbal medicines to local physicians. In other words, I gave everyone what would please them.

At that time I received a letter from the king of Tsang in western Tibet, sent by urgent courier. The letter said:

"This Himalayan land of Tibet is in immediate danger of invasion by an extremely large Mongolian army. Great vidyadhara, the time has come for you to arrange interdependence in this matter with all the ability you can muster! History will record whether you, the king of mantradharins, had or did not have magical power based on this moment, so please do something about this immediately! I am offering you a hundred loads of barley via the castellan of Dakpo Nangwa; please send monks to count and receive them. The castellan will also supply you with whatever else you need."

As requested, I arranged interdependence in many ways – outwardly, inwardly, and secretly. Just by my doing so all the Mongolian forces dispersed like clouds struck by stones, as everyone has heard.

The Mongolian prince Choghtu Khong Tayiji sent me a letter accompanied by twenty-five auspicious scarves and four bolts of brocade – in all, five sets of ninefold offerings. I dedicated his merit and prayed for him, and wrote back to him, sending him samaya substance, protection knots, and supports for his faith.

Although I was engaged in ongoing efforts to interdependently repel Mongolian invasions, look at how much faith Mongolians had in me! This can only have been due to Guru Rinpoche's compassionate blessing. It's a good thing I'm such a humble person; otherwise, if I were one of those who consider themselves a great lama, I might claim that these events were signs of siddhi! Ha ha!

Another Mongolian leader accompanied by four attendants offered me two farms in Kyimo Valley in Shoka. Then another one requested me to pray for him at his death; this happened in the western Longpo district in Kongpo.

The king and queen of Maryul sent me a load of saffron with a request that I perform divination on their behalf. I clearly saw all their doings of the past, present, and future, and advised them on that basis. They gained extremely great faith in me.

A kusulu from Jang Barong Rock came to see me. He had dispensed with all the concerns of this life, and was a person able to utterly disregard food, clothing, and conversation; a true king among practitioners with real bone in his heart. Someone for whom day and night were unceasing luminosity, he had received a prophecy from dakinis in a visionary dream, and having heard my story, abruptly left his retreat to come meet me. I taught him the essence of my terma dharma, and he returned to the uninhabited wilderness from which he had come.

All of these events occurred within a couple of months. Around the same time a few Indian yogis came to see me; I ripened them with terma dharma.

Samdrup Kyi, a property owner from Powo Yegong, offered eighty-five measures of pure silver in sponsorship of the accumulation of six-syllable mantras by the sangha of Bangri; this amount would equal twenty-five loads, if converted into tea currency. At Tawa Tsakung in Kongpo, through the sponsorship of Lama Drakpa Gyurmey and the donor Samdrup Kyi, we accumulated a hundred million six-syllable mantras. Along with this was a rainfall of profound dharma. The valleys were filled with empowerment and transmission. The sun of teaching rose. The ocean of instruction swelled. Such a large number of people were in attendance that I could only display the empowerment implements and let them file by to receive the touch of a silk cord.

Then another donor from Yegong, a woman named Sheltrengma, offered another large amount of silver in sponsorship of six-syllable accumulation. I gave it, along with the tea and butter we had received, to Padma Tendzin, our monastery's manager, to serve as a means of our purchasing grain. This time we accumulated the six syllables right here at Bangri.

At Tselagang, Taktsang Dowo, Jomo Jong, and other

places I performed ritual services including protection and reversal and gave authorizations as requested. At Gurzang I was able to restore a damaged temple as commissioned by the local leader, whose name was Senge.

At that time Shapdrung Tendzin Rinpoche, the fourth rebirth of Tendzin Nyima Zangpo, the son of the siddha Tangtong Gyalpo, came to Bangri from central Tibet with a few disciples. I offered them the empowerments, transmissions, and instructions from my new termas. In particular, I offered them many additional profound dharmas of the Nyingma tradition, such as the vidyadhara Vulture Feather's terma *Great Perfection: Penetrating Wisdom*, the *Peaceful and Wrathful Deities*, and the *Eight Dispensations*.

Then the precious dharma lord Mipam Tashi Lodrö, like a lamp running out of oil, dissolved his mind into the dharmadhatu; none of our efforts to improve his condition were successful in preventing it.

My mind and all it encountered filled with sadness, I entered strict retreat for five months, living alone in my room. Unable to sleep even in the middle of the night, there was a constant ringing and buzzing in both my ears, an empty sound that seemed to fill the whole area. No matter what I thought about, it made me even sadder. Both the precious dharma lord Mipam Tashi Lodrö and the Shapdrung of Daklha Gampo reappeared in my mind constantly. Uncontrollable tears flowed steadily from my eyes. Other than praying to them earnestly there was nothing I could do. In order to refresh my recollections of the precious dharma lord, I wrote a short account of his life.

Although most of his many followers, yogis and nuns alike, devote themselves to the accumulation of bad karma by denigrating me, I put up with what they say about me. I don't know if it would frighten them if I responded in word or deed; I just know that my forbearance has not caused any of those base men and women to feel so much as a sesame seed's amount of faith in me.

The precious dharma lord was a king among renunciates, Vajradhara in person; why are so many of his followers demonic? I've often pondered this.

I spent my days transcribing terma parchment and my nights practicing sadhanas of Guru Rinpoche's mind; at least this brought me the ability to trust myself.

Soon after that the Gyalwang Karmapa Chöying Dorje visited Kongpo, staying at Tselagang. I wrote him a letter, conveying homage and requesting his permission to visit him. In response he wrote me back:

"To the dharma lord and tertön: It is my intention to receive you here as soon as possible. Wait a little while; we will soon be reunited."

This first letter was accompanied by generous gifts of an auspicious scarf, tea, and grain. I continued to stay alone and received another letter, which said:

"Dharma lord, tertön: I am writing to tell you that it is likely that I will becoming to your area; we will see each other then. Please keep this in mind!"

Soon thereafter the Karmapa went to Shokha; his route brought him very near Bangri, so I and my disciples welcomed him with our best attempt at procession and with prostrations. He dismounted his horse to receive our prostrations and accepted our offerings with his own hands before passing them to an accompanying official. Casting barley grains of consecration at Bangri Tashi Öbar, he gazed intently at it and asked questions such as, "Tertön Rinpoche, is the water here agreeable to you?" He also cast grain at the Bangri sangha.

When the Karmapa continued his journey I accompanied him in attendance. I also offered him all the meat on my ribs, as we say: eleven silver auspicious scarves, a hundred and thirteen measures of gold, fifteen weights of silver, a palm-sized coral, a large turquoise, three male horses, a bright copper pan, a cloak, a canopy, a curtain, sets of both flat and hemispherical cymbals, tiger and leopard skins – all together, seven sets of ninefold offerings, although it feels pretentious to call my shoddy gifts "offerings." At the same time we presented him with a few provisions for a ganachakra: enough that it took fifteen people to carry them. He accepted our offerings with evident great affection.

Once the Karmapa reached Shokha, I was summoned to his retreat house there and offered him several extraordinarily sacred termas, including the scepters of Guru Rinpoche himself – a golden vajra, a silver bell, an iron kila, a coral vase, and a wheel of meteoric iron – as well as an amazing, extraordinarily fine spirit-stone of the terma guardians, and the text of the *Glorious Intersex Protector*.

When I placed these before him, he abruptly rose from his seat, took three steps forward, accepted them with his hands, and placed them on his head, closing his eyes and praying. Then, staring at me, he asked me a lot of questions. Finally, he said, "You have real merit! You are the guru of most of the gurus of Tibet!"

He then gave me an auspicious scarf one fathom in length; three horses along with their tack, including a fine antique saddle decorated with gold and stirrups decorated with amber; a cast image of Amitayus; a cloak of gold brocade that he had worn himself; his own fine tea cup with an ornate Chinese stand; a silver bowl; a curtain; a canopy; and bolts of woven fabric such as cotton and silk. He was extremely generous.

To the sangha of Bangri he gave horses, copper pans, and cymbals – nine of each. He also sponsored tea service, which he has done repeatedly over the years. In his compassion, he has really cared for us.

Because of the Karmapa's presence in Kongpo many people gathered there from all over, even coming to our new little monastery at Bangri. I was amazed by the sheer volume of visitors to my monastery. I got quite tired of it but made myself stay there, although there were times when I thought I couldn't stand it any longer.

People came all the way from Nepal, Bhutan, Ngari, southern and northern Latö, Lhodrak, central Tibet, Jang, Nyal, Lorong, Jangshap, the six districts of eastern

Tibet, Powo, Yegong, and the three districts of Kongpo; in short, they came from just about everywhere – pilgrims, people requesting dharma, those who simply wanted me to pray for them or establish a connection, and even a great number of people who just wanted to be touched by my hands or feet, or just see my face and hear my voice.

I gave so many empowerments and authorizations that the bottom of my empowerment vase became worn through and had to be patched with new silver. This is not a lie; it really happened!

Even more recently, last year and this, a great number of people have come here from great distances to form a dharma connection with me or request my prayers. From Tsurphu Monastery I received a letter and offerings in request of my prayers for Gyaltsap Rinpoche's recently deceased bursar. From central Tibet I received a letter and offerings in request of my prayers for Chakzam Shapdrung's deceased mother. From Yarlung I received offerings in request of my prayers for the Nesar Jedrung. From Tangpoche I have received two letters from Chöje Trechung.

I've received letters accompanied by offerings from all sorts of major, intermediate, and minor lamas stating their wish to be entrusted with my terma dharma, such as Zuri Lama, the nirmanakaya of the supreme siddha Lingrepa, Gyatön Chöje, the Derge siddha Palbar Trungpa, Katok Lama, Atra Lama, Tsetsam Kukye, Gar Tulku, Latö Jangpa, Karak Tulku, Chögowa, the king of

Biri, Lutsen Namkha, Bönpo Lama, and the nirmanakaya of Aryadeva.

Many monks have come here continuously from eastern Tibet. Some have stayed; others have returned to their region, greatly increasing the benefit to beings of terma dharma.

Led by the leaders of Zapuk Seat in Tsang, the Nyingma lamas of Tsang such as those of Kakashar together invited me to that region, giving precise reasons why I needed to go. Unfortunately, I was unable to.

Shokha Nangso is the foremost civil and spiritual authority around here, and is the only one we trust up here at our retreat. I have offered him both the finest things I have and all manner of ritual service, and he has held us in his compassion. No one else has been able to be as supportive to us. When salt became scarce his officials donated salt to Bangri and also gave a great amount to me personally.

Nowadays, no matter where I go I cannot escape the presence of lots of people. Still, I found myself not wanting to stay here at Bangri and fled with two disciples to Gurzangpu; we were unable to remain alone even there. We went to an even more isolated spot called Sremo Ugyen Guru, but still could not realize our hope for solitude.

If I could be alone for just one month in an empty valley free from the barking of both humans and dogs, fragrant with rhododendron and juniper, and graced by the sweet call of ptarmigans my wishes would be fulfilled, but compelling circumstances prevent even this.

After failing to find true isolation, I thought to myself, "Because I'm old now, it seems that I'm unable to go anywhere without a horse, and that I need the help of at least two other monks. It also appears that no matter where I go people will still find me. Since I find myself forced to share in the common misery of human society, it seems that I will have to just buck up and stay here at Bangri regardless of whether I like it or not!"

However, even at Bangri people with attitudes in accord with dharma are rare. So many people come here now!

If I eat I'm unable to digest my food; if I don't eat, sleep escapes me at night. If I don't pay enough attention to people they denigrate me, but when I try to conform to their social expectations I find that my faculties have diminished with age and that I find company even more disagreeable than I did in the past.

My mind is torpid. I'm forgetful. My eyes are unclear. I'm going deaf. I'm getting lazy, uninterested in doing anything. Even the sound of a good voice irritates me. I'm unable to walk on my own feet or write with my own hands. So many of my teeth have fallen out that I'm unable to speak clearly, and I can no longer remember what I've said. My mind is so torpid that nothing I do has any order to it.

All this seems like more than mere defects of age; I've wondered if it might be a sign of impending death, or if I've become enveloped by some terrible obscuration.

If you think about it, the opportunities of this life are gained only once, and this life is momentary, as short and cold as daytime in winter. Whether you give material things away or get them, they all disappear.

Oh, managers of monasteries: It is said that generosity is the king of practices. Ensure that none of the sangha's goods go to waste! Don't let them spoil in storage! Don't allow even a single grain of barley or wheat to be lost, a single spoon of flour to be spilled, a single chunk of salt to be wasted, or a single drop of tea or beer to be spilled! Everything offered to the sangha must end up in the mouths of the sangha.

As for the sangha: Never waste your time in gossip! Devote yourselves to dharma practice and the pure performance of authentic ritual practices. If all of your mantra repetition is performed in a state of natural, undistracted mindfulness, all of your sponsors and everyone who fetches your water and gathers your firewood will complete the accumulations and purify veils. Keep this in mind!

Otherwise, if the sangha concerns itself only with its own pleasure, greedily stuffs offered food into its mouths, guzzles down donated beverages, and throws out whatever it can't swallow on the spot without any recognition of the expense incurred by donors, it will have become utterly foolish. Such behavior is nothing more than ignorance of the results of actions.

What is offered to me out of faith is always the most donors can give – they break earth and crack stone to give it, as we say – so it is not something that just anyone can digest without severe karmic repercussions. I therefore plead with all you managers: Be wise! Be careful! Be thrifty!

Up to now none of the major, intermediate, or minor offerings made to me by faithful donors have gone to waste; they have all been used to sponsor images of body, speech, and mind in general and especially the manuscript reproduction of one hundred and seventy copies of the several volumes of these new termas.

Also, in the service of the Buddha's teachings a community of the sangha, whether large or small, is indispensable. For its foundation there must be a temple where the sangha may gather. The creation of such new temples and monasteries is only possible through the donations of laypeople.

In particular, since the Nyingma vajrayana teachings are nowadays like the sun about to set behind mountains, I have used offerings made to me to sponsor the creation of dance costumes, such as masks and cloaks, and even feast beer and tea distribution for the Tenth Day festivals. I have sponsored debate, composition, and practice; and made sure all that was donated and sponsored reached the mouths of the sangha.

Through Guru Rinpoche's compassionate blessing within a span of ten years the gathering of monks and disciples, the making of the uniforms of sutra and tantra, and the institution of ritual practice with correct melodies have all occurred spontaneously.

I could summarize my life as this: Since my eleventh year and up to now I have never been without my medicine bag. There are always sick people, so I have always had to prepare so many medicinal formulas that I'm always tired of doing so. On top of that I have had to prepare so many protection amulets and samaya substances that I am extremely tired of that too. By this point in my life I find even giving empowerments and authorizations and teaching dharma irritating. It would be fine with me if there were a limit to the demands made by male and female donors!

In order to resolve disputes among villagers I have had to contribute horses, yaks, dzos, tea, and fabric, and there is an endless line of beggars at my door. The people around here are audacious; they don't see me as a source of dharma but as a source of material goods. When they're sick they beg me for medicine; when they lack anything they beg me for it; when they quarrel they beg me to resolve it; when they burn themselves they beg me for burn medicine; when they get married they beg me for silk and cotton; and when they sew clothing they beg me for decorative additions.

The powerless demand food and clothing. The powerful demand taxes. Monasteries demand ceremonies of accomplishment and offering. Monastic colleges demand tea distribution. Pilgrims demand soup. Beggars demand service. Everybody, even brewers, boatmen, and the guardians of roads and bridges, sees me as a source of acquisition.

I may not have many disciples, but I do sustain a sangha. I make offerings and give generously, and will do so until I take my last halting breath.

Here in Tibet all other dharma traditions flourish no matter what they do, but Guru Rinpoche's followers are always at a disadvantage. Seeing this, although a butterfly cannot hope to fly through the reaches of space, I have tried to assist our tradition as best I could, thinking that it is better to gnaw on turnips than go to sleep hungry. I suppose this is nothing more than the faith of ignorant sectarian attachment on my part.

Of course, how could I alone sustain the teachings? All my monks and disciples need to work hard as well. Nevertheless, Jetsun Milarepa said:

> Straight trees without knots are rare.
> Flawless, perfect people are rare.

As he said, when some people look at my monks they see signs that they're not thinking about holy dharma. It starts when they say, "We need to build huts." Once they've built them, they influence one another until they start drinking beer. That exhausts their supplies, at which point they say, "We think we should go on a pilgrimage." Or, they claim to be ill and, wishing to drink "medicinal water," they say, "We must go soak in the medicinal hot springs." A great herd of them wanders off together. They head for nunneries, drinking beer as they go and telling lies until the immorality of one has turned a hundred of them immoral. Eventually they get tired or sick, and remember their monastery.

Such monks, while living in the mountains, hanker for the villages. Unable to study or practice sadhanas, they forget even the practice of tranquility meditation, and gossip endlessly about who got what and who lost what. Once any two such monks are in the same place their tongues start to wag. They waste their entire lives but are utterly unaware of doing so. After their deaths their corpses are eaten by dogs. Most monks are like that.

Oh, I am depressed, sad to the point of weeping! There is a saying:

> Falcons, mousehawks, and owls
> May make their nests in the tops of the same tree,
> But their intentions are different.

The saying is true; if someone has no karmic predisposition for holy dharma from previous lives, they may practice dharma for a while in order to conform to the expectations of a well-behaved lama or their own parents, or they may think of dharma for a while under the influence of companions, but eventually they will destroy themselves. The vidyadhara Suryachandra said:

> I am not a practitioner merely because I couldn't
> feed or clothe myself,
> Nor was I driven to it by enemies or demons,
> Nor am I merely too sick to do anything else;
> I am a practitioner because the thought
> of death is in my heart.

I am a practitioner who entered dharma's gate
as a well-loved child.

As what he said there implies, most of the dharma practitioners around here are "devoted Buddhists" because they are incapable of any real work. The kind of monk that suits me is one who requires no more than a full belly and enough clothing that he doesn't freeze, and on that basis studies, meditates, and does virtuous things to the best of his ability. Even if all he can do is repeat the six syllables a hundred million times, he will have made good use of his human life.

The ornament of a practitioner is learning. The sources of a practitioner's satisfaction are morality and accomplishment. What practitioners need is to help beings.

In other words, I would be delighted by monks who behave in accord with dharma; keep to a modest position; wear ragged robes; maintain the external conduct and appearance of bhikshus while practicing the highest vajrayana; let food, clothing, and conversation take the loss; and recognize whatever happens as the compassion of the three jewels. If a few good monks who always wear their monastic skirts properly and gracefully and their shawls with dignity, who constantly and quietly repeat the six syllables, who desire little and are content, and who are really in accord with dharma were to appear I would be delighted. Even if I had to run around performing ceremonies in villages to support them I wouldn't have a hair's worth of regret. Unfortunately, due to the times we live in, such monks are rare.

Instead, we have monks who drink beer, quarrel with one another over rank and position, are jealous, and forget all about dharma as long as they can accumulate donations fit to break the earth and crack the rocks. Not only do they ignore dharma, they quarrel and fight.

When offerings are meager they say, "This monastery has no disciples; we must go where wealth is plentiful!" If their lama scolds them even mildly, they say, "This insult requires retribution!"

When I see such communities I can't help feeling that the lamas who have many monks, if they have long lives, will eventually be surrounded by a vast herd of samaya breakers, and that there is no certainty that holy dharma will not cast them into lower rebirths. Oh!

Latsewa, my precious dharma father, wrote:

> All the elders I once knew are gone.
> New people unknown to me have come.
> Spending one's life in materialistic distraction
> Is too sad!

While my monks will never be wealthy no matter where they go, they will never be poor. The donations we receive include horses, copper armor, flat and hemispherical cymbals, cloaks, bolts of silk and cotton, felt, tea, butter, rock salt, spices, boot soles, rope, cloth patches, and needles and thread. All of this is equally distributed. At some monasteries monks can't be sure they'll receive a supply of tea every year! When I was living in the presence of the precious dharma lord Mipam Tashi Lodrö we thought it was a big deal to receive even a meditation belt and hat!

People who think are rare. I have done everything I could for my monks: prepared medicine when they were sick, performed rituals for their benefit, given them edible yantras, and fumigated them. When they've died I've carried their corpses, ejected their consciousnesses, prayed for them, and devoted myself to virtue on their behalf. There is nothing more I could have done. It is said that those with eyes of wisdom, present in the unmanifest expanse, see the truth.

Anyway, what's to be done? My liking for monks has decreased. Especially, when I see bloodshot-eyed monks who like beer or a flock combining yogis and nuns, I feel deep dislike in my heart. However, since all space is filled with karma and kleshas, people like me are in the minority.

If I don't explain this no one will understand, although even if I explain it a hundred or a thousand times some people will still not understand. In the Buddha's authentic words it is clearly taught that, without holy dharma, every other pleasant or unpleasant endeavor is utterly pointless. I've understood, experienced, and realized the truth of this. My eyes have seen sickness and pain. My ears have heard birth and death.

We really must practice holy dharma! We really must keep our vows and samaya even at the cost of our lives!

People say that nuns and other women provide needed service and, in the long run, are fine vessels for the vajrayana, but for monks on the path female company is like poison, for it leads monks to behave disgracefully. The vow of chastity is very important.

Monks who like beer claim to see spirits; they think their claims serve to inspire people. I think that very little faith is produced by the example of drunkenness; certainly people without an inherent predisposition to faith will only be repulsed by it.

However, if I imposed my standards on monks I wouldn't have any; as long as they abstain from sex and liquor, whoever wants to come here is welcome!

Anyway, I know how to handle them, like using one tooth to eat when you've only got one left in your mouth. If you're surrounded by a lot of monks and you let them do whatever they want, it will end in disaster for everybody, so I've had to employ a great deal of pacification, enrichment, power, and violence while guiding monks.

I've argued with some, expelled some, hit some with a stick, thrown ashes at some, and thrown some out after giving them a little money. I have supported some only with food and clothing. To some I've taught dharma. I've fought with some. In other words, I've done everything I could to ensure that, even if they don't become perfectly dharmic, they don't get reborn as something nasty.

In some cases I've just cut their hair and let them be donors. In other cases I've pleased them with gifts and protection knots, then caused them to have faith in someone else. I've done all sorts of things, as appropriate to each case, in order to guide them.

Even so, given these times, the karma, kleshas, and habits that people bear make them very hard to tame. Bad karma is vast, samsara is deep, and suffering is extensive. When people are so bound by the knots of delusion, there isn't much you can do for them. No matter what holy dharma you teach, people are like leaky vessels; immediately afterward they return to their previous behavior.

Oh, guru, three jewels, hear me! If I wanted to practice dharma in a way that would make me happy, I could be happy anywhere. Even if I were accompanied by a few disciples, I could still manage to be happy. It is my hope to help everybody and benefit beings that prevents that, although I think that much benefit is unlikely.

Put another way, there is no one at this retreat who could tell me what to do; no one here is my guru. I'm as free as a mushroom in the forest. If I decided to leave today and go to live alone in a cave somewhere no one could stop me. I have complete autonomy. As my faculties are diminishing with the loss of youth, I've started to wonder if I've finished benefiting all the beings I'm going to in this life.

If there's anyone who will listen to me, hear this: Maintain the noble behavior and robes of at least a shramanera. Whether you are learned or not, live out your life in isolated retreat and silence. Have few desires. Be content. Even if all the practice you can do is to repeat a hundred million six-syllable mantras, you will have fulfilled my wishes. Everyone, please keep this in mind.

The greatest Nyingma tertöns of the past held, protected, and spread the Buddha's teachings. They were unimaginably great; there were many such revealers. The intermediate ones were only able to renew the dharma of termas. The worst revealers were not only unable to help beings; many of them couldn't even protect their own lives. There were even some who fell under the power of liquor and sex; their behavior was worse than that of ordinary people.

My service to beings has not been especially vast or elevated, but I've managed to preserve my independence; I've never listened to what people say. I have maintained the purity of my samaya with all the lamas with whom I've formed a dharma connection. I have also, through aspiration, arranged the interdependence for an unceasing stream of emanations until samsara is empty.

Well, that's about all; that is the story of what I've done for beings from the time of my white-toothed youth up to the present time of white-haired old age. Samaya!

Oh, the good I've done beings in innumerable
  past lives,
Based on the two accumulations, is inexpressibly vast.
Thinking of it makes me sad.
I remember eleven Indian lives
And twenty in Tibet, this dark land.
I remember many lives elsewhere among the
  six states.
These memories are vague, dreamlike.

I don't tell everyone about them because few would believe me.
To speak only of this karmic birth,
My awareness was clear in the bardo of becoming.
While dwelling in my mother's womb
All appearances were pure in bliss, clarity, and nonconceptuality.
The first year after my birth was quite unpleasant.
Then good habits reasserted themselves.
In my eighth year I began to study sutras, tantras, and shastras.
Starting in my sixteenth year I helped beings through medicine.
I gave up all immorality, even common songs.
From my twenty-first year until my fortieth I was immersed
In undifferentiated day and night, generation and completion.
From then 'til now, when I'm fifty-four,
I've tried to help beings in ways that suited each of them.
If I die now I'll have no regrets.
Shakyamuni, Vajradhara, Padmasambhava,
Songtsen Gampo, Gampopa,
Gyalwang Karmapa, and Mipam Tashi Lodrö:
I, Bangriwa, am an emanation of them all!
My names are Letro Lingpa, Jatsön Nyingpo, and Humnak Mebar.
I've written these memoirs freely, without falsehood.
If there's anything wrong with them I apologize.
If I've any faithful followers, keep them in mind.

Chapter Four: 1640

OM MANI PADME HUM HRIH!

Lord Mahakarunika, Arya Avalokita, hear me!

There is a clear prediction in my termas that an obstacle to my life is going to arise in my fifty-fifth year – this year – so last year I gave extensive advice and guidance to my monks and disciples, marked the covers of all my books with their titles, and wrote a list of all my samaya substances and herbal medicines so that none of them would fail to be identified after my death. I returned to their owners everything that had been lent to me and gave away everything extra I possessed, except for things unfit to give anyone and a lot of what I had written; those I offered to the god of fire.

Soon after that I began to have bad dreams. The toothaches and dropsy from which I already suffered have worsened, and a number of new symptoms of illness have appeared. There is nothing I can do other than pray to my guru and the three jewels. Some people have suggested that I have ritual services performed for my benefit; others have wanted me to summon a skilled physician. This is my response:

"OM MANI PADME HUM HRIH! Lord Manakarunika, hear me! As for the commissioning of ritual services, all my wealth and possessions have already been offered to the three jewels or fed to the mouths of the sangha. None of the donations I've received remain; none have gone to waste. I now possess only my three robes; aside from those I am free from the snare of possessions. There could be no better ritual service for my benefit than for you to use all extra food and beverages as offerings or in generosity to the needy. People say that the miserly should practice generosity, that the obscured should practice confession, and that those who dig in the earth and break rocks should make ransom offerings. I have no idea whether such services would help me, but I think that the bad karma I've accumulated in past lives is being purified now.

"As for physicians, I know my own condition as well as any other physician could. They say that of the four hundred and four ailments only a hundred are curable by physical medicine, and that there isn't much a physician can do about merely apparent, imaginary, or dependent illnesses.

"I am not denigrating interdependence or ritual

services, nor do I lack faith in them. The lord protector Jikten Sumgön wrote:

> In the face of what is good, arrange profound
> interdependence.
> It is sufficient for you to create perfect conditions.
> In the face of what is no good, apply the remedy of
> reversal meditation.
> This is the instruction on how to expose the lie
> of relative truth.

"In accordance with what he wrote, you should all recite liturgical practices of pure dharma. In particular, just repeat the six-syllable mantra, for it is the best ritual service there is. Whether what is happening to me is a result of past karma or of present conditions, if the six syllables don't help me, there is no way that "HUM HUM PHAT PHAT!" will!

"The Buddha, the victor Vajradhara, Guru Padma, and all the sutras, tantras, and upadeshas have taught above all the benefits of the six syllables. In particular, Avalokita is the destined deity of Tibet. In addition, he was the indisputable yidam of King Songtsen Gampo, the peerless Gampopa, and the holy refuge Mipam Tashi Lodrö. The deity to whom I have totally entrusted myself is also Arya Avalokita, the King of Space. So, everyone, please recite OM MANI PADME HUM."

We have performed a number of services for my benefit: numerous MANIs, a hundred thousand hundred-syllable mantras, a hundred thousand *Heart Sutras*, a hundred thousand Amitayus dharanis, and a hundred confession and fulfillment liturgies.

I have moved my bed to the northeast side of my room, and altered other aspects of the geomancy of my dwelling according to the great perfection teachings and those on retreat in general. I have created a small shrine to the right of my bed and a small protector shrine to its left; those have really helped. Unfortunately, there are still many obstructive forces arrayed against me. Several of my monks have died, funds have dried up, and a lot of people have gotten sick. There has been no way to prevent all this.

Of course, I'm not alone in this. We all reach a time at some point in our lives when we can't help wondering if we wouldn't be better off dead, but are unsure whether or not we're about to die. When someone indispensable to us dies, we are utterly unable to prolong their life. Because of the infallible results of actions, we all experience some degree of agony at death; I've seen that.

Although I've received many donations, I've done my best to purify the resulting veil. I plan to continue unembellished meditation until my last breath as best I can. I feel that there is no need for any other special services for me, and that there is no need to summon a physician; I'm a better doctor than anyone else around here.

As always, my dream would have been to die peacefully in an isolated place, free from the barking of humans and dogs, fragrant with rhododendron, filled with the sweet calls of ptarmigans; however, it seems that our hopes are one thing and our lives are something else.

Whatever happens, I'll be okay. Everything I possess must go to my monks; other than that I've no concerns. There is no need to offer so much as a needle and thread to any other lama or any other monastery in request of prayers for me after my death; I have already offered a little to each of my many lamas. I have already erected supports. My wishes are already fulfilled. I have dedicated my body as an offering, so after my death cremate me and offer the fire and its light to the three jewels.

If this little monastery of Bangri survives it will help the region of Nyangka and especially this locality, but I don't know what will happen. Monks who've come from distant places won't be able to stay, but if a few local monks can hold out here, because of the tremendous blessing of this place they will definitely achieve supreme and common siddhi. I promise to return to this monastery on every tenth day of the lunar month.

It is irritating to die before my karmic lifespan is completed, because every day I'm alive I progress incredibly. I'm also irritated when I think of the suffering of taking a new body. However, no one can stop the sun from setting.

All my followers: Practice holy dharma with fortitude; there's no point in anything else you might do. My only other remaining instructions are written on a little scroll within my copper amulet.

If I don't die now, I will continue to teach dharma, give empowerments, and provide instructions. I also have much more profound terma to disseminate should indications arise that it is time to do so.

I conclude with the interdependent aspiration that I survive and be able to add to these memoirs. Those with faith, please keep all this in mind.

I prostrate to the three jewels.
If I, the tertön of Bangri, die now
I won't have the slightest regret.
I remember many past lives.
I see what will happen in times to come.
There is value in recounting my memoirs;
It is not pointless nonsense.

Drogön Gyalse wrote:
"Write your will while your mind's still clear.
Eat a funeral feast while it's fresh.
Meditate on your guru while his image is clear."
That's what he wrote. In that way
I've written my memoirs before my death.

In this life through study I've learned enough
To reveal the true meaning of the sutras and tantras.
As for my inner meditation experience,
I've seen the boundless expanse
Beyond acceptance and rejection.
The extent of my realization is to understand
The nature of things beyond apprehension.
I've helped all beings by displaying

Miracles and signs of siddhi.
I've become the guru of all Tibet.

When I traveled I rode in procession.
When I sat they seated me on a lion throne
With a canopy, curtains, and incense.
They adorned me with robes, cloaks, and silk cords.
They held parasols above me and carried banners.

I was surrounded by a sangha of monks
Wearing robes and ceremonial hats and playing
music.
Their melodious chanting was inspiring.
I taught dharma, gave empowerments, and showed
people their minds.
Our dancing and costumes transformed perception.
Donors and disciples gathered like clouds.
Undefiled experience bloomed.
I helped beings through drawing mandalas,
Protection, reversal, and termination.

I held the teachings of Nyingma vajrayana.
I established the practice of the Dakpo Kagyu.
I'll have no regrets if I die now.
Mara of death, come right now!

I will relax as my life dissolves.
When death is very close
And earth, water, fire, and air dissolve
My mind will be like a candle in a vase,

For I've understood that lucidity and emptiness
are inseparable.

Vajradhara himself has said:
"Death is just a concept we apply
To the journey to the celestial state."
When appearance, increase, and attainment occur
I'll have no fear or trepidation.

Even if I fall unconscious for three days
It will not be a problem, because
Penetrating wisdom is unobscurable.
Then, when consciousness and appearances resurge,
Water will mix with water, light with light,
Fire with fire, and wind with wind.
As light and rays of light,
Outer and inner space will mix.
How could that be called a "bardo"?

Natural forms, sounds, and rays of light
Will be great ornaments of nonduality.
In Abhirati, Sukhavati, and Chamaradvipa
Your son will certainly join his father.
Rishis, vidyadharas, and dakinis
Will certainly receive me.

I am joyous and unafraid to boast.
This illusory body has many ailments.
No matter what I've done it makes me suffer.

When my breathing stops I'll cast aside its burden.

I will pass from bliss to greater bliss.
All disciples with faith in me,
Pray to me then; you'll profit.
No matter what realm I reach
My compassion and blessing will grow.
Whatever your aspirations, they'll be quickly
accomplished.

Some will think, based on their outlook,
"The dharma lord tertön has died!"
Really, there is nothing in the mind that can die.

Gampopa wrote, "Your mind
Is beyond beginning or end.
What is there in it to die?
One thought follows another.
What is there in them to die?
If an illusory city's destroyed,
What is there in it to die?
When interdependent things separate,
What is there in them to die?
When the colors of a rainbow fade,
What is there in them to die?
If you sustain ordinary mind,
You are inseparable from me.
Once you understand inseparable lucidity-emptiness,
You become inseparable from me.

Once you understand appearances and mind to
be one,
You become inseparable from me."
He wrote that; keep it in mind.

If I don't die in my fifty-fifth year,
I'll have more instructions to give.
I'll have more to impart to disciples.
I'll have more holy dharma to teach.
I'll have more to write about my life.
I'll have more profound terma to give.
Repeatedly pray that I do.

Chapter Five: 1640–1642

OM AH HUM!

OM MANI PADME HUM HRIH!

That year we did a great number of ritual services in order to dispel our superstitious belief that I was about to die. This exhausted our financial resources and used up most of our possessions. However, as they were spent on offerings and generosity I've not so much as a hair's worth of miserly regret. I managed to continue unceasingly all of my daily meditation practices. I also received from Tangdrok Tulku Rinpoche the empowerment from Padma Lingpa's terma the *Vajramala Ayusadhana* a hundred times as well as much other dharma I'd not previously received. I pleased him with offerings that were not too meager.

To everyone involved in performing ritual services for

me I offered whatever I had and provided them whatever service I could. By the end all I had left were my three robes.

The indications in my dreams improved steadily; in one dream I saw a steep rock face on which was a spinning red swastika, a sign of longevity. I became more hopeful, and my various ailments lessened in severity. Many signs arose that other obstacles to my life were deferred: three of my cups broke; my dog died; two horses were lost; one of our buildings was destroyed; and seven monks died. As for me, I had a nosebleed that didn't stop for nine days.

The fact that in spite of all these obstacles I didn't die that year must be due to the compassionate blessing of the three jewels.

I think that if the great leaders of communities and all the greater and lesser lamas asserted to be learned and accomplished would engage in means to prevent further Mongolian invasions it would be more meritorious than the recitation of billions of MANIs; it would certainly help the unprotected people of Tibet tremendously.

We deceive ourselves with our petty sectarianism. As a result, we only practice dharma to make ourselves comfortable; no one is engaged in the means of repelling the adversities that threaten all Tibet.

I possess a great deal of interdependence, but if I did what I want I don't know what people would say; they already say all sorts of things about me. The armies of the eight classes of spirits have approached me secretly many times out of purely benevolent concern, but the paucity of beings' merit in these evil days prevents a fortunate outcome. Oh, guru, three jewels, hear me!

When I reached my fifty-sixth year a large number of people gathered here, coming from all over this land. In particular, the dharma lord of Paro, Bhutan, came with an entourage of fourteen disciples. They made hundredfold offerings and also presented more than five hundred bolts of cotton. I offered the dharma lord some especially fine terma substances, the three dharma robes, a ceremonial hat, one of my teeth (which had conveniently just fallen out) as a support for his faith, and a not too meager sum of other things. I gave all of the empowerments and transmissions of the new terma.

Then a lot of people came from Katok Monastery in eastern Tibet, Lhodrak, Latö, Tsurphu, Rechung Cave, Gyatön, Alangö, Nyewo, Powo, Riwoche, Sakya, Drikung, Tsaritra, Tsokar, Chikchar, and Sengtam. Bönpo Lama came with his disciples. In other words, people came from everywhere, some all the way from Dartsedo and China.

I gave the *Collected Sutras*, the *Mani Kabum*, the *Heart Essence of Vajrasattva*, the *Heart Essence of the Dakinis*, and many other empowerments, transmissions, and instructions as requested by various people. I repeatedly gave the entrustment of the complete new termas, and wrote instructions, dedications, and aspirations as requested.

At Dingtang we convened an accomplishment

assembly of the *Peaceful and Wrathful Deities: Emptying the Depths of Hell.*

I taught, bestowed empowerments, and performed retreats. I traveled all over this region, presiding over assemblies. In one month alone I performed seventeen major public empowerments. I received lots of offerings.

Then, for about six months, a steady stream of pilgrims – male and female, monastic and lay – appeared at my door. Each day there were at least three or four of them, usually around fourteen or fifteen, and sometimes as many as thirty.

Some of them would say things like, "May I just look at your face from the doorway? I know it's too much to ask for your touch!"

In such cases I would reply, "That won't do; this must be your first pilgrimage. As I bear the title 'lama,' it is my duty to serve you; at the very least, I must bless you with my hands, cast blessed grain on you, and make prayers and aspirations on your behalf, however briefly. Given that you've traveled a great distance and climbed over high mountain passes in order to get here, if you were prevented from actually meeting me it would sadden you and hurt me as well. If I failed to welcome you, I would be at fault; I have no choice."

I've given some pilgrims a kilo of barley flour, others just a bowl of it, and at the very least I've given them all enough to drink that their thirst is quenched, as well as a samaya-substance pill. I've conversed at least briefly with each of them; good manners require as much.

At the same time, I'm tired of opportunistic beggars who know they can depend upon me to feed them. The saying "compassion ends in anger" has some truth to it. However, I've never turned anyone away empty-handed. I've made offerings and given gifts to some; given tea or beer or whatever food I could to others; and given at least a protection knot, samaya pill, or edible yantra to each. At the very least I've blessed each one with my hands and spoken with them. I have never turned anyone away out of arrogance or a sense of my own status.

Of course, as I've already written, if I could die quietly in an isolated hermitage in a juniper forest graced by the pleasant sound of flowing streams and the sweet calls of ptarmigans my wishes would be fulfilled. It seems that this is not going to happen; given my age, I've accepted that I won't be able to fulfill that wish. Also, when you compare it to the hardship of traveling all over this land, living here at this retreat is fairly comfortable; no matter where you go, you'll never find a place that attachment, aversion, and the other kleshas haven't reached.

There was a time not too long ago when some maras took the form of monks of this region and, along with some greedy community leaders, some yogis who were evidently demons in disguise, and other demons in the form of nuns, said that I'm not really a tertön. A lot of people accumulated the karma of saying a lot of things that were and still are untrue.

They are embarrassed these days. Even though they've acquired human bodies, with full freedom and tremendous opportunities, they haven't done anything virtuous; they haven't even repeated a hundred MANIs! Instead, they denigrate people. I feel sorry for them.

All you who discuss whether I am or am not a tertön, look at my activity!

By this time, because of the interdependence of the external and internal, the clouds above Bangri had begun to take the form of the faces of wrathful deities, peaceful deities, or semi-wrathful deities. Some were in profile, some had three faces, and some had animal heads. Some clouds took the form of letters and syllables, or images of mind such as scepters, or offerings, or the eight auspicious signs and substances. Even the shape of the earth, mountains, snow, trees, and rivers appeared in various visionary forms. I had the experience that they were all speaking to me.

When I was alone, such as when going to sleep, I saw myself as actually surrounded by many companions. I wondered if these might be signs that virtuous spirits were trying to request dharma from me and vowing their protection. Sometimes a single day and night would seem to last many nights.

When people with faith were coming to see me from a long distance I would see them in my mind as clearly as though it were with my eyes around a day before their arrival. I saw the five poisons of those in whom they were strong as clearly as a reflection in a mirror. If someone heavily obscured was coming to see me I would feel weak and tired, and sleep poorly. I saw all of the spirits that came along with offerings as vividly as if they were physically present; I repeatedly had to give them substitutes and banish them. None of this was proper supercognition, but it was a definite sign that my veils were somewhat diminished.

At this time I clearly recognized the supreme nirmanakaya of Dakpo Norbu Gyenpa, as everyone has heard or seen by now.

Then I said to Padma Tendzin, our manager, "You are overworked; you've served me faithfully and diligently for seventeen years without respite. Next year will be your obstacle year; go into solitary retreat and repeat mantras and meditate as much as you can. As they say, it's best to get up right after a good dream!" I gave him images of body, speech, and mind, and lots of other presents.

I then said to Khyentse Yongdrak, "From now on, for better or worse, the responsibility is yours. Do your best!" I think that, due to the compassion of the three jewels and my merit, we'll be fine. I could have found someone more generous, but who knows how they'd turn out in the long run? I'm not very trusting.

I've given many community talks to my monks that go like this: "We must all entrust ourselves entirely to our gurus and the three jewels. Our tantra is the *Recitation of Mañjushri's Names*. Our shastra is Gampopa's *Ornament of Precious Liberation*. Our liturgical practices are the *Five Royal Sutras* and the *Seven Chapters*. Our deities are Mahakarunika and the peaceful and wrathful forms of Guru Rinpoche. Our view is the great perfection. Our meditation is mahamudra. Our conduct is whatever accords best with the vinaya. Try to live your whole lives in silence in retreat."

Then I entered my fifty-seventh year. I taught and gave empowerments in Kyenang, and received invitations to several places, including Daklha Gampo and the southern borderlands. As I was followed in my travels by many pilgrims from Katok and other places in eastern Tibet, our presence became a burden on the local people.

I received a letter from the king of Jang accompanied by offerings. Five other people from Jang came to me with offerings as well. The dharma lord of Tingting also came to see me with his disciples.

The Shapdrung Khenpo of Tashi Tse, the nephew of Nesar Jedrung, came from central Tibet with twenty disciples. He and his entourage had made the journey on foot, and brought elaborate hundredfold offerings with them. I received the entrustment of the Sakya Path and Result from him.

With so many people coming to see me I had to provide food for more than two hundred and fifty.

I once more gave the empowerments, authorizations, transmissions, and instructions of the new termas at the Shapdrung Khenpo's request. During this time he said to me, "Due to the times we live in, there are few siddhas like those described in the teachings left in central Tibet. This is because there is more emphasis on looking good, on the cultivation of reasoning, and on the size of monastic establishments. You often hear people talk about the number of monks in a monastery; they say, 'There are two hundred monks there!' 'There are three hundred monks there.'

"We concern ourselves with melodies and fine ritual, or study and teaching. I've not seen anyone I really believe in. That is why I've come here to receive your profound termas."

I replied, "What you say is true. Our practice of the Buddha's teachings is deteriorating. Given that they have disappeared from India, the source of holy dharma, and are deteriorating in central Tibet, how could things be any better here in Kongpo?

"Among authentic lineages, I see the Karmapa and his sons, and the Drukpa, as the most amazing. There is a vast amount of terma dharma, but nowadays the terma of Padma Lingpa and Shikpo Lingpa have the shortest lineages and the noblest of origins. Otherwise, things are as you have said."

Upon my return to Bangri Lama Tenpa Dargye and his disciples came bringing extensive hundredfold offerings from eastern Tibet. These included seven hundred horses and mules, all bearing full loads of other offerings. He offered my sangha both a tea distribution and a silk distribution. As he was one of my monks I gave him all of my recent termas and all that he had not previously received. I also created the interdependence for his helping beings by giving him a set of the three robes and images of body, speech, and mind.

I then received another letter and offerings from a Mongolian prince; I sent him blessing substances and an image.

Once again a very large number of people from all over the land gathered around me. I thought, "There is no one to help me greet all these people; I have to do all the talking myself!" The thought of this made my mind tired.

Now I give each pilgrim a cup of weak beer and a single samaya pill. One time I was unable to even bless pilgrims with my hands. My attendants weren't going to admit some of them in fear of contagious illness; I told them to let it go.

Although I'm a lama, I have nothing tremendous to give people as presents, and what good do the offerings made by pilgrims do? As soon as one pilgrim has left the door of my retreat two show up to take their place! This endless line to my door irritates me. No matter where I go I can't escape the crowds; I'm tired of it. I pray that, if I'm born human in my next life, I spend my entire life in strict retreat, practicing until the day of my death without involving myself in human affairs, and dwell in undifferentiated day and night and lucidity-emptiness. Guru, three jewels, hear my prayer!

Oh, if I think about it, I doubt whether I'm long for this world. Why? I've exchanged samaya with so many people, malevolent spirits are especially spiteful now, beings' merit is weak, and we are threatened by invasion; in particular, Mongolia's breath is steaming hot. I think

I'll die soon. It is no doubt only due to the compassion of my guru and the three jewels that I've survived this long and done so well.

No matter how you think about it, without holy dharma everything is like a dream or an illusion. If you consider wealth alone, I started out with nothing more than my three robes. I had no fine food, nor even a single extra garment. Then, at one time I had three hundred measures of gold; five hundred of silver; four hundred loads of tea; strings of coral, amber, and turquoise; and a hundred bolts of brocade. All of that was used to make offerings to the three jewels and to support the sangha; it's all gone now, but I've never felt so much as a hair's worth of regret. Nowadays the gifts I give and the offerings I receive are pretty much equal. I see this as an obvious demonstration of impermanence and illusion. Oh, everything, absolutely everything, is just like that!

It's said that if you want to achieve buddhahood in this life, and you pray to a guru whose lineage is noble and prominent and who possesses all outer and inner virtues and qualifications including longevity, blessings will automatically enter you. However nowadays, aside from a few scattered siddhas, lamas who live up to their lineage predecessors in renown and benefit for beings are extremely scarce. Even worse, the lineages of samaya-breakers and the demonically possessed are nowadays the most celebrated. It seems that our own fortitude is no longer enough. No matter what beings do in such bad times, there is difficulty.

If you consider this, it is obvious that those with the good fortune to encounter these profound termas should be conscientiously diligent. Unfortunately, most lack the merit and get lost in indolence. It's sad.

Lately, I've gained even more faith in the value of OM MANI PADME HUM as a way to discipline mindfulness. I've committed myself to repeating at least twenty thousand of this mantra daily, although I've sometimes failed to do so.

Wealth and possessions go against holy dharma. In addition, receiving many donations definitely brings sickness, pain, disputation, and gossip. When you're hungry, dry flour tastes as sweet as sugar; when you're thirsty, cold water quenches your thirst better than anything else. When you're neither hungry nor thirsty, even if you drink clarified butter it will just nauseate you.

These days I've no taste for many guests or many monks. I'm happy as long as I can just not deviate from my old regimen of meditation sessions. I don't wish to acquire more wealth or possessions, nor to increase my benefit of beings. Fame, progress in meditation, supercognition, signs of attainment, material things: I've no need for any of them.

My body is not going to get any younger. My white hair and wrinkles are not going to diminish. My eyesight and memory are not going to improve. I don't know how many more years I'll live. If I die peacefully, without terrible agony, my wishes will be fulfilled. However, let whatever comes come. I can put up with disappointment.

From my white-toothed youth up to my white-haired dotage I've not done anything, not so much as a hair's worth, that I need regret. Guru, three jewels, see me!

The learned Zurkharwa wrote:

> Never defer the repayment of kindness; repay it promptly!

Accordingly I've always given male and female donors, monks, and friends whatever I could as soon as I could. I've never procrastinated or left it for "tomorrow" or "some future time." It's better to repay debts; what good does hoarding a lot of stuff do?

Lord Yutok wrote:

> Don't let enemies be; subdue them skillfully!

Accordingly, in the state of bodhichitta, and merely through arranging interdependence, I've happily and auspiciously subdued those who view me with antipathy and wish me ill. I've symbolically squashed some with earth until they were neither alive nor dead. I've drowned some in water; they've gotten extremely sick. I've burned some in fire; they've died immediately. I've cast some to the wind; they've moved far away. I've fed some to protectors; they've died in a timely manner. I've performed sutra rituals for some; they've become maddened by spirits. None of them have come to happy ends.

Lord Padma Karpo wrote:

> I prostrate to you with whom all connection
> is beneficial!

Accordingly, many of those who pray to me have mixed the expanse and their awareness. Some have mixed day and night. Some have devoted themselves to sadhanas such as longevity practices, the six syllables, or the peaceful and wrathful forms of Guru Rinpoche. Many of those have repeated millions or hundreds of millions of mantras in retreat. I've helped others through ransom rituals, divination, medicine, causing rainfall, preventing hail, and preventing epidemics.

Many of my monks have helped others as well and returned to me with hundredfold offerings in gratitude. Others have continued to practice in strict retreat. Many of them, having died, have been reborn with recollections of their previous lives.

Who could count the number of empowerments, transmissions, and instruction I've given; or the number of people I've taught to read, write, and chant; the number of people to whom I've taught liturgies or the MANI mantra; the number of people who've vowed before me to abandon wrongdoing and practice virtue; or the number of animals whose lives I've saved?

After my death, my followers will continue to do well; they will not regress. People of the future: look at all this!

The biographies of some lamas are written by monks very attached to them. In such cases the minor virtues of the subject are invariably exaggerated, multiplied four-fold or fivefold. I've even seen biographies based entirely on oral accounts of the subject's life. Here, I've written of my life without concealing anything, good or bad. I felt it was fitting to do so because my disciples asked me to.

Nowadays I have seen many who call themselves bhikshus but have no vows; who call themselves tantrikas but have no magical power; who call themselves meditators but can't bear retreat; who call themselves "beyond action" but are filled with desire; who call themselves siddhas but exhibit no signs of siddhi; who call themselves spiritual friends but don't know how to teach; who claim to have mastered their energy yet produce bastard children; who claim to have mastered meditation yet have no patience; and who merely wear the costume of a Buddhist while utterly wasting their lives.

From the prophecies within *Mahakarunika: Self-Liberation of Lower States*:

> In Kongpo, the melodious sound of MANI PADME
> will resonate.
> Everyone will gain faith in virtue.

This prophecy appears to have been fulfilled now. There are many MANI stones, carvings, and prayer wheels around here nowadays. Also, the number of village tantrikas who recite the *Seven Chapters* and sadhanas has increased.

Through the power of the Gyalwang Karmapa,

Kongpo has become so peaceful that an elderly woman could safely travel alone while carrying gold. There was a time when everyone revered yogis alone. As a result, everyone who was lame, deaf, or sick; every widow and widower; every poor villager who couldn't pay their taxes; and every other desperate person put on the costume of a yogi and would gather flocks of people. Similarly, women unable to find husbands would pretend to be nuns, but invariably fail at dharma. This whole region was impoverished. Cholera and other diseases were so prevalent that it seemed the human race was going to die out. Crops were carried off by the wind, leaving an arid desert behind. I used to wonder what was going on. If you compare those days to the present, we are all pretty comfortable nowadays.

At first, as hard as I tried, there were constant obstacles that threatened to carry me off. Then, just by my meeting the Gyalwang Karmapa, everything I wished for began to happen. His compassion and blessings are greater than those of anyone else.

Of course, some people say, "Each of us must guard our own tradition." There are three types of faith: the faith of awe, the faith of aspiration, and the faith of belief. Entrusting oneself to one's own ignorant sectarian prejudices, however, is not the faith of awe.

If you pray to whomever you trust the most, blessings will come to you; that is the nature of blessing. Someone who practices holy dharma because they recollect death should follow their own faith and practice the most profound instructions available to them; it is not like civil or political allegiance or loyalty. Those who say "I will receive dharma from no one else" are merely displaying their own arrogance and wrong views. It is a case of what is meant by the saying, "If you eat food from a dog's mouth you will shit dogshit." Sadly, because of the times in which we live, misguided allegiances proliferate.

I think that there are a few people who accord with dharma and want to come here to Bangri; I've dreamed of a lot of gold being found in the ground, and that even the weakest practitioners discovered a measure of gold every day. One night I dreamed that each member of the sangha at Bangri received a large measure of gold. I've had a lot of good dreams about Bangri, and improved the interdependence of this land by erecting stupas and so on.

I attended a large ceremonial gathering of Karma Kagyupas at Shokha Nangso. When I prostrated to the assembly and circumambulated it, the sangha there displayed an extremely great pure outlook toward me. I think the reason all Karma Kagyupas like me so much is the interdependence of my sincere faith in the Gyalwang Karmapa.

When the Drukpa Rinpoche Paksam Wangpo dissolved his mind into the dharmadhatu I received offerings with a request for my prayers. I wrote a reply and sent offerings to his remains of gold, silver, and a hundred bricks of tea; I sponsored the making of offerings for three weeks after his passing and offered my prayers.

Then I went to Daklha Gampo. I found the nirmanakaya of Lord Norbu Gyenpa to be brighter than crystal, whiter than a conch, more beautiful than a rainbow, and utterly authentic and trustworthy. He clearly said that he recognized me. A precious image of Gampopa had spoken to the nirmanakaya; it said to him:

> Welcome, nirmanakaya of the unsurpassable guru!
> Ripen and liberate beings as
> This image of me prophesies!

The image spoke further, invoking a command seal.

I cut his hair and offered him the name Gyurmey Dorje Gyaltsen; that name was kept secret for a while. I made the aspiration that he gradually receive the vows of refuge and a shramanera and arranged that this occur. While there, in the context of a brief amrita accomplishment assembly, I offered him every empowerment, authorization, transmission, and instruction, pouring the contents of my vase into his. I also offered him all my material possessions.

Many people gathered at Ganglung to receive dharma from me, so I gave the complete new termas. A rainbow appeared, as well as many other wondrous signs. On my way back to Bangri I formed many connections through prayer and aspirations. When I returned to Bangri Tashi Öbar I was pleased to see that everyone there was in retreat. I offered them each profound instructions in accordance with their individual needs.

KARMAPA KHYENNO!
OM MANI PADME HUM HRIH!

Right now the days and nights are comfortably warm. The mountains and valleys are green. Rainfall is adequate but not excessive. We are without blight or hail. The crops are good and plentiful. There is no fighting. There are no epidemics among humans or animals. The grass is lushly green. Birdcalls are sweet. The fragrance of incense is fine. Our offerings are well arranged. My monks accord with dharma. Children are learning their letters. Elders are meditating in retreat.

When I see all this, if I can manage not to die for a few more years, I will enjoy life and feel happy, with clear awareness. With none of my deeds straying into wrongdoing, in the dharmata mandala of bodhichitta beyond outer and inner, in the state of the natural, spontaneous, unaltered great perfection, I sip black jasmine tea from a white porcelain cup. Living like this is definitely due to the compassion, blessings, and siddhi of Padmasambhava of Uddiyana. In the boundless purity of all that appears and exists; the immeasurable equality of everything; the precious wisdom of buddhahood, I feel truly happy. E MA HO! A LA LA! KYE HO!

These are my memoirs up to my fifty-seventh year.

Part Two

Wondrous Light:
A Brief Account of the Final Days of the Vidyadhara Jatsön Nyingpo

I bow at the feet of the glorious guru skilled in
sending down the rain
That dispels the anguish of existence and nourishes
the flowers
Of benefit and happiness, born from the clouds of
wondrous activity
Inseparable from the compassionate wisdom expanse
of all victors.

From the fine vase of white lapis that is his life,
The greatest feast of vast and profound holy dharma's
ambrosia,
I will recount here his final deeds.
Listen, those with faith and strong yearning.

The innumerable magical bodies, names, deeds, realms,

and array that all embody the compassion of victors and their children and will do so for as long as existence lasts, these endless displays of guides for those needing guidance, are beyond description and the limits of an ordinary being's understanding. However, in absolute truth, they are all without exception of a single nature: they are all one in the single great sphere, the lord of our family, the vajra master. Therefore merely hearing, seeing, or recollecting the name or any of the deeds of that supreme embodiment of all victors, our peerless guide, frees us from this terrifying ocean of existence and sets our feet on the good staircase to great awakening. He is so meaningful that he should be our only thought.

The genuine refuge, protector, support, and friend of desperate, miserable beings in this final age of fivefold degeneration; this holy, noble, glorious lord of all mandalas; this peerless possessor of the compassion, wisdom, love, power, and might of all Buddhas was called Jatsön Nyingpo or Ugyen Letro Lingpa.[16] The banner of his fame flies over the peak of existence.

16. Fivefold degeneration is the degeneration of life, emotions, beings, time, and views.

The feast of his memoirs includes his outer memoirs, which he wrote for all of his disciples and recount his well-known deeds; his inner memoirs, which are his collected songs and advice, written to satisfy the wishes of various individual disciples; and his various secret and very secret memoirs, written to serve as jewel-like sources of inspiration and blessings for those most worthy who possess samaya. All of these were written by this lord himself; they are extensive and detailed. Copies of them are now all over this ocean-covered world.

Here I am going to briefly recount the end of his life, his final deeds in this realm, and how he demonstrated the magic of parinirvana.

Buddhas and those on the levels of supreme siddhas are not menaced by birth and death. They have transcended the entire system of composite apparitions. They no longer possess the causes or conditions of change. They will never revert to a state of fluctuation, transformation, loss, or destruction.

Ordinary, deluded beings are shrouded by the darkness of ignorance. We are possessed by the demon of incorrect concepts. We have contracted the chronic illness of karma and kleshas. We have poisoned ourselves with bad habits. We therefore never feel even a moment's interest in meritorious endeavors or the lifestyle that brings liberation and awakening. We exhaust ourselves with our obsessive craving for the types of negative, samsaric actions and behavior that perpetuate our deluded fixation on relative truths. Food, clothing, possessions, profit, reputation, schemes, plans, enemies, friends, attachment, hatred: although all these things are more dreamlike than dreams themselves, we fixate on them as real, distracted by our ferocious, obsessive delusion.

In order to turn our thoughts away from this, show us the composite as it really is, and lead us to give rise to the desire for freedom and the accumulation of good habits so that we turn toward liberation and genuine reality, awakened beings display apparent parinirvana. This is one aspect of their skillful activity. All Buddhas of the three times finally display it.

Our guide in his youth donned the armor of diligence through fierce feelings of sadness and an intense desire for freedom. The way in which he practiced both elaborate and simple meditation with unvarying discipline is hard for ordinary people to fit in their minds. All his songs and written advice spur us on our way in dharma by reminding us of renunciation, impermanence, and the fact that we have no time to waste.

Whenever people like me who are numbered among his disciples met with him he spoke only of how he was not going to remain long in this world and how we needed to arrange the interdependence for his longevity and perform rituals for that purpose. When we offered him images of longevity he clearly accepted them only to fulfill our wishes; he always appeared unwilling to assume his own survival.

The prophecies in his termas regarding his lifespan say that if he had lived to eighty his activity for the benefit of beings and the teachings would have been even greater than it was. However, the good fortune of beings in this age of dispute and especially of his disciples was insufficient. The interdependence allowing him to reveal all of his profound termas did not arise. In particular, this tertön had a dharma cycle concerning the achievement of the rainbow body that was extremely profound.[17] If the interdependence for its revelation had arisen it

17. This is the *Heart Essence: Self-Illuminating Dharmadhatu.*

would have had an important effect on his lifespan, his followers, and his lineage. Sadly, he did not reveal it due to the shadow cast on him by a few samaya-breakers.

In other words, because the collective merit, of beings and the teachings, was insufficient in numerous ways, he did not live to the age prophesied in his termas.

A few years before his passing he became slightly afflicted by dropsy. Because he saw all appearances as illusory he left his illness and the concept of illness in the unaltered natural state of his realization of equal flavor. He didn't accept any medical treatment or engage in any alteration of his regimen. When it reached the point where his attendants, other ordinary people of this age of dispute, and the rest of us could stand it no longer, we petitioned him, saying, "As you, lord, are a master of all branches of medicine, please accept whatever medical treatment and alteration of your regimen will alleviate this illness."

He replied, "As you say, I know more about these things than any of you. Because of the nature of the composite and our individual karma, we don't get everything we want. I've already offered all my wealth and possessions to my guru and the three jewels; there's nothing that they don't know or don't see. What more is there to do?" He answered our request in such ways, and didn't listen to anything we said.

When he was approaching the age of sixty there arose terrible turbulence all around us, violent and disturbing changes in our society.[18] He responded to these events

18. This refers to the repercussions of the invasion of 1642.

by showing a demeanor of even greater renunciation than before.

Since he dwelled in the great equality and primordial purity of samsara, nirvana, the three times, outer, inner, and other, he was incapable of pleasure or pain or of the deluded concepts of good and bad, but he demonstrated those deeds that would best benefit those beings of these ending times most strongly fixated on permanence.

In those days every letter he wrote me and others was like a testament or will. He wrote:

"People like me support ourselves dishonestly by heedlessly consuming donations; we dare to call this 'service of the teachings.' We adopt the guise of lamas yet devote our lives to everything that contravenes dharma and concern ourselves with this life alone. This is horriic; everything about the way we live is fit cause for regret. I rejoice in your living in an isolated hermitage. It's important that you stick to that! That is how our forebears in the practice lineage lived. I think that I am on the point of demonstrating impermanence. I've given away all my possessions: offered some to the holy, given some to my peers, and given the rest to the needy. Having nothing to which I could be attached, I'm as free as a bird!"

He distributed his possessions among various monasteries, lamas, and disciples, giving each what was most appropriate. This was an inconceivably fine display of impartial generosity. From then on he remained in retreat, meditating.

By the time he entered his sixty-second year his illness

and his resultant water retention had become so severe that he was no longer able to rise from his seat. His attendants and entourage became unhappy and found the situation intolerable, but this lord remained impassive and continued to spend his time in meditation. He displayed no sign of being in pain, not even for an instant, and sat with his legs crossed and his gaze unwavering.

Two of his main disciples, an older lama and a younger one, offered him a mandala and supplicated him insistently, saying, "Lord, you have control over birth and death. For the good of all beings throughout space, and especially out of your love for the monks and disciples who depend on you, please look upon us and remain alive! If you must depart out of consideration for disciples in other realms, please tell us where your emanations will appear, and in what form? To whom shall we pray?"

Because of the nature of the composite, and because he had completed his guiding of disciples in that body, he did not consent to remain. He said, "I will not be reborn here. Nowadays the times are so bad that even if I were reborn here it's unlikely that I'd be of definite benefit to beings and the teachings. There is no point in reincarnating in these dregs of time. All of you, be diligent in holy dharma; whoever practices dharma properly will be inseparable from me."

He instructed us in that way. Although the older tulkus and lamas who were his disciples had all received all of his termas, some of the younger ones had not, so he gave them entrustment and blessing using his *Record of Received Teachings* and other books. He also gave audiences to his nephew and some major donors, giving them his final advice and instructions at length and fulfilling their respective wishes. He also gave kind dharmic advice and gifts to other monks and disciples individually.

Earlier in his life this lord told me, "After my death, you must take care of Bangri, my seat."

I replied, "As I am utterly uneducated in either the mundane or the spiritual sense, I am unfit to direct a large community. Especially, given the uncertainty of the time of death, at this point in my life I'm only interested in being in retreat. I've decided never to involve myself in the direction of a monastery."

He didn't accept my refusal, but responded, "Such uncooperativeness will not do! You must, no matter what, maintain the summer dharma and winter dharma and ensure that the succession of the teachings continues.[19] If after my death my seat were to be adopted by one of the greater monasteries it would be easier for everyone, and from a worldly point of view probably more successful, but a humble place that accords with dharma would be better. Especially, I think it is essential that we preserve an independent lineage of Nyingma vajrayana."

Although he spoke that way to me several times, later on, toward the end of his life (a time by which I was already in retreat) all his letters contained remarks like these:

19. Summer dharma is the rainy season retreat undertaken yearly by all Buddhist monastics. Winter dharma is a yearly period of intensive debate and study.

"I said those things to you in the past, but without pure and holy dharma, there is no point in the mere name of a seat. No matter how you look at the times we live in, there's no point in my causing obstacles to your practice of dharma. It's best if you emulate the lives of our Kagyu forebears."

Similarly, when speaking to his nephew and various attendants he said, "Given these times and particularly our dharma emphasis at Bangri, the situation here, and the prophecies concerning this place, everyone who lives here after my death must emphasize the practice of holy dharma. Distractions such as keeping up appearances through elaborate funeral services for me, the creation of images, and the so-called 'preservation of my seat' are unnecessary." He spoke in ways exactly like the testaments of siddhas of the past.

A few days before he died he sent me a letter by courier telling me to come to him. Unfortunately my health did not allow me to make the long journey; the interdependence for me to see the mandala of his face again in this life was just not there.

He entered unfluctuating samadhi. In that state, at midnight during the eleventh month of the Male Fire Dog year he demonstrated the dissolution of his rupakaya into the expanse of mahamudra, the immaculate wisdom of unchanging great bliss, the dharmakaya.

Oh, you, beings' protector, are beyond fear
Of bondage, liberation, birth, and death.

Decadent beings like me have no protector.
Abandoning us, god of gods, where have you gone?

Sun without shadows, king of light,
You've no concept of near and far.
Why have you deserted us in this
Vile darkness of karma, kleshas, and obscurity?

Why have the brilliant rays of your wisdom and love,
Peerless in might, disappeared from the sky they once filled?
Tireless, how can you abandon beings as long as they exist?
I pray that you illuminate the good path for your disciples.

Guide, emissary of the victors,
You dissolved, for a time, into the expanse of peace.
This vast earth and its oceans shook then.
All beings and the gods wailed in grief.

Camphor, saffron, and jasmine fell as rain,
Covering the earth with their blooms,
Turning this world into the Potala realm,
Alleviating our grief and pain.

Rainbows of splendid color formed canopies,
Banners, parasols, and auspicious designs,
Filling the sky beyond limit like
The divine wealth of Indra.

A mild southern breeze brought
The fragrance of sandalwood,
Its fine scent lasting all day and night
As a devoted offering to you, supreme victor.

The stream near your seat suddenly became a river
Of cool, refreshing water, its surface adorned
By flowers like bunches of pearls.
They too were an offering to your remains.

Those finest of lotuses, your emanated disciples,
Gathered quickly around your residence.
The drums of their throats roared in the music
of prayer.

Although winter had begun in Tibet,
The earth all around stayed soft and warm.
At the end of each week flowers fell as rain;
Like snow, they adorned the ground.

Wondrous signs of all kinds appeared in the sky
Up to the peak of existence, and all knew that you,
victor,
Had passed beyond suffering; they offered and
prayed.

In this lord's will, he wrote:

"Keep anything special that occurs surrounding my death secret for as long as possible; there is an interdependent reason for this. Seven years would be best;

failing that, seven months; at the very least it is important that you keep these things secret for seven days."

They were unable to conceal the rainbows and other signs any longer than seven days. Then all his monks and disciples gathered whatever offerings they could and began a continuous assembly of prayer and aspiration. Offerings were made to his precious remains for two and a half months. They also made offerings to all of the larger and smaller monasteries in central Tibet, Dakpo, and both the south and north of our land. Especially, they presented elaborate offerings for the interdependence of their aspirations to holy persons and other lamas and spiritual friends; most of them observed a week of services.

Then, on the eighth day of the month Phalguna, the virtuous occasion of Shakyamuni's birth, they escorted this lord's precious remains to their cremation stupa. Fueling the fire entirely with white and red sandalwood and aloe, his assembled disciples, led by the tulkus, performed a fire offering to his remains.

They had sent repeated invitations to me via courier, but circumstances did not allow me to attend, so I set forth whatever offerings I could in my retreat hut on the day of the cremation and imagined that they were fire offerings. In that and other ways I did what I could in veneration of and service to him.

On that day, while the assembled monks, disciples, male and female donors, and others with faith were prostrating and making offerings to his remains, a tent and lattice of rainbows adorned by various shapes and colors appeared from the southwest, ending above the cremation stupa. The wonders seen by those present that day are too many to recount; they corresponded to the worthiness of each individual. They all saw a piece of his skull disappear; it was never found, and so everyone says it was taken by wisdom dakinis. His heart, tongue, and other wondrous relics were preserved in a reliquary. His will asked that some of his ashes be poured into the river and some brought to the peak of the mountain. When this was done the river suddenly grew; it is said that his ashes remained visible, floating on the river's surface, for three months. It is also well known that later on the small pieces of his bones that survived the fire produced many miraculous images and relics. An excellent image of Humnak Mebar and entourage was cast from copper and gold.[20] It was filled with his blessing supports as well as the three types of relics. Radiant with blessings, it resides at his seat, emitting its magnificent goodness.

The greatest of victors Letro Lingpa,
Jatsön Nyingpo, Humnak Mebar:
By many names he is known in all realms
As the lord of all mandalas.

For the good of beings in Tibet in these dregs of time
He appeared and displayed miraculous deeds.
His life was an ocean of wonders;

20. Jatsön Nyingpo was given three names in his termas. His outer name, Ugyen Letro Lingpa, means Tertön With a Karmic Connection to Guru Rinpoche. His inner name, Jatsön Nyingpo, means Rainbow Essence. His secret name, Humnak Mebar, means Fiery Black HUM.

This account is merely a drop on a blade of grass.

Yet by my writing it, may his followers gain trust.
May the faithful remember his kindness.
May all who see or hear this be freed.

For these reasons, and to complete his
    autobiography,
Ugyen Tendzin Sönam Palzangpo,
A great being born from this lord's dharma,
Rich with hearing, thought, and meditation
    through past training,
Asked me, Natsok Rangdröl, to write this.

Led by this pure virtue, I dedicate all the good
    I've done,
Composite or not, throughout every life,
To the fulfillment in the immaculate expanse
Of this supreme refuge and victor's intentions.

The wondrous lives of victors are pools of jewels.
They grant the wishes of the devoted and dispel the
    heat of existence.
In them grow the fine seedlings of higher rebirth and
    the lovely flowers of liberation.
They are the delight of wise young swans.

I've no learning or wisdom; my mind is dull.
My foolish writing couldn't please the learned,
But telling the truth about this victor's deeds
Is not wrong; it can only lead to good.

I therefore ask that you ignore my poor words
And, with devotion, consider their meaning.

Seeds of wheat are small and yet their fruit
grows high.
Like that, may my good intent in writing this
Cause me to become the collector of the teachings
Of all victors, and benefit beings.

By all the wealth of goodness and excellence
In victors' realms as many as atoms,
From now until samsara's end,
May the victors' teachings, joy, and richness fill
all worlds.

On this good day in the waxing phase of the month Chaitra in the Water Snake Year, I, Natsok Rangdröl, wrote this with devotion by the bright light of the moon in the hermitage of Vulture Ledge Cave at the sacred place Palrigong on the eastern edge of Kongpo.[21] By the virtue of this may all beings throughout space quickly achieve the state of the supreme and noble lord guru. SARVA MANGALAM!

21. The Water Snake Year of 1653 C.E.

Part Three

From the Embodiment of the Three Jewels: A Brief Account of the Tertön

NAMAH SATGURAVE!

Padmasambhava, beings' only refuge,
Is indivisible from my root guru.
Therefore, with unfabricated devotion,
I prostrate to him in every way.

From now on in every life
May my guru's compassionate blessings
Care for me without a moment's separation.
I request of you the siddhi of great equality.

This is the story of the vidyadhara Jatsön Nyingpo, a mind emanation of the yogin Nyangben Tingdzin Zangpo, blessed by the great master Padmasambhava in many lives.[22]

He was born at Baru Namtsal in Kongpo under the

22. Nyangben Tingdzin Zangpo was a disciple of both Padamsambhava and Vimalamitra, and the principal heir to the latter's teachings on the great perfection.

constellation Pushya in the Female Wood Bird Year. Because of good habits from the past he was devoted to dharma, and learned to read in his third year just by being shown the letters. He thought only of fleeing to dharma; he tried to do so many times, but was unable to get away.

In his eighth year he met Trungpa Sönam Zangpo, a great disciple of the Gyalwang Karmapa. Sönam Zangpo advised the tertön's parents to have their son study medicine. As a result, he did so from his twelfth year until his twentieth. During those years he dreamed of Guru Rinpoche on every sacred occasion.

No matter what he did, Jatsön was constantly sad and earnestly sought genuine dharma, so in his twentieth year he succeeded in fleeing to dharma in the presence of the glorious Mipam Tashi Lodrö, a great bodhisattva who has taken successive rebirths for the good of beings, an emanation of Prince Lharje and Chengawa Gomrin.

At the time Mipam Tashi Lodrö dreamed that some women brought him an old stupa built by Guru Padma and asked him to repair and reconsecrate it. When he did so it became brilliantly radiant.

Jatsön Nyingpo fled the world and became a shramanera in his presence. He also received vajrayana empowerment and the name Ngawang Chögyal Zangpo. He then immersed himself in one pointed cultivation of the true meaning, practicing diligently. At various times over the next few years he visited Daklha Gampo, met the omniscient Drukpa and the peerless Lhatsewa, undertook completion, and received much dharma.

He then went to the isolated site of Bangri Jokpo, vowing to practice there for thirteen years. While one-pointedly engaged in practice he had repeated dreams on sacred occasions of the Ninth Gyalwang Karmapa Wangchuk Dorje, who gave him advice and instruction on progress and correction of flaws in meditation. These instructions may be found elsewhere.

In other dreams and hypnagogic experiences Jatsön repeatedly encountered a woman who prophesied to him that he would open the door to hidden valleys and reveal several termas. Unsure whether these experiences were signs of siddhi or of an obstacle, he consulted the precious dharma lord Mipam Tashi Lodrö, who told him, "This is definitely not an obstacle, but it is important that you keep all this secret from others for a while."

When Jatsön completed one hundred million Vajrapani mantras, on the tenth day of the first month in the Earth Monkey Year, light rays shaped like trumpets repeatedly radiated from his eyes, illuminating the upper and lower sites where terma was concealed.[23] He clearly saw the terma locations, like when sunlight reflected on water shines on rock. After this had happened several times, he started one night to explore these locations, but was frightened off by the abysslike gorge he would have to cross to reach them, which was filled with a turbulent river and fierce wind.

He followed a less intense light ray to one of the locations. Digging through the rock, he discovered a treatise

23. Some editions of this text, as well as other sources, give the Metal Monkey Year instead of the Earth Monkey Year as the time at which these events took place. The Earth Monkey Year was 1608; the Metal Monkey Year was 1620.

called the *Practice of the Four Common Preliminaries*, which we believe to have been previously discovered by Sangye Lingpa and then reconcealed by him.

Jatsön then made a second attempt to reach the principal terma location. He fell into the gorge; his injuries were not too severe.

Every night thereafter he dreamed of a woman repeatedly showing him the location of terma. Finally, he reached the site and spent an entire day there.

He first found a cast iron garuda the size of a small bird's chick. Inside it was the index of termas, in the handwriting of Yeshe Tsogyal. As directed by it he made the requisite offerings to the terma guardians. Then, in the twelfth month of the Monkey Year, almost at the beginning of the Bird Year, he rappelled down the rock face and found three stone markers. Under the top one was a reliquary amulet sealed with wax. Inside it he found the twenty-three scrolls of the *Embodiment of the Three Jewels*, in the handwriting of Nyangben Tingdzin Zangpo, consecrated by Guru Rinpoche, and concealed by Yeshe Tsogyal.

Under the second marker he found a triangular clay reliquary containing samaya substances, an image of Amitayus, and the water of life. Under the third marker he found objects to be offered to the Tenth Gyalwang Karmapa Chöying Dorje; as enjoined by the terma index, he left those where they were until the signs of it being time to remove them arose.

For twenty-five days Jatsön remained unseparated

from the parchment scrolls he had found. He offered a hundred prostrations, a hundred butter lamps, feasts, and tormas. Praying sincerely to Guru Rinpoche, he transcribed the scrolls. He has told me that, at the time, he was worried that if he didn't finish the transcription and reconceal the original scrolls within one month it would damage the local environment and immediately bring other undesirable consequences.

Since then he has discovered many other indices of profound terma and prophecies; it is fit that the stories of those discoveries be included with each respective dharma cycle.

Because the dharma lord Mipam Tashi Lodrö identified me as the predicted single root among the prophesied twenty-one root and branch heirs to this dharma; because I was exhorted in dreams and hypnagogic experiences; and because of the interdependence of the words and samaya substances of this terma, I invited the vidyadhara to Daklha Gampo upon his completion of fifteen years of intensive practice. All of the auspices surrounding this were excellent. When this dharma was placed in my hands as its heir a tent of rainbows emerged from the southwest, ending above my retreat hut. Everyone present saw this, as well as the deities, scepters, auspicious signs, and rain of flowers that miraculously appeared then.

I've no doubt that Jatsön Nyingpo will continue to reveal more profound terma without impediment; his extraordinary qualities are exactly as prophesied in the *Radiant Prophecies*.[24]

24. The *Radiant Prophecies* are part of the *Embodiment of the Three Jewels.*

This account of the discovery of the *Very Profound Embodiment of the Three Jewels* was written by me, Gampopa Mipam Chökyi Wangchuk, exactly as described to me by the tertön himself, on a good day in the eleventh month of the Water Pig Year.[25]

25. Gampopa Mipam Chökyi Wangchuk was one of the names of Dakpo Norbu Gyenpa. This Water Pig Year was 1623.

In these days when the teachings are waning,
It's very hard to tell dharma from nondharma.
I've seen many fooled by fake terma.
Some have found authentic terma
But violated time-signs, auspices, or samaya,
And fallen prey to obstacles; I've seen that
many times.
Because I've slightly turned my mind
To the study of all manners of art
I'm arrogant and hard to convince.
I've tested this profound dharma like gold,
And have found no fault in it.
I've also seen evidence of its natural blessing,
So I believe in it and want to practice it.
Those who angrily denigrate this simply lack
A connection to Guru Padma's compassion.
May this *Very Profound Embodiment of the*
Three Jewels
Spread in every direction and flourish.
May the longevity and activity of its holders increase.
May it bring all beings to supremely great bliss.
MANGALAM!

Part Four

Jatsön Nyingpo's Visionary Journey to the Glorious Copper-Colored Mountain:

An Extract from his Secret Memoir: Visions of Boundless Purity

When I completed the outer, inner, and secret sadha-nas of that profound terma I offered a hundred feasts. Many extraordinary signs arose, and my body became so engulfed by bliss and warmth that I sweated and steam rose from me.

When I went to sleep that night, I dreamed that I went to a place where many women were dancing. Among them was a bhikshuni; she was clean, had fine features and form, was wearing the three dharma robes and a red pandit hat with long earflaps, and holding a begging bowl. She said to me, "Beyond this land is the wondrous realm of Guru Padma. Do you wish to go there? If so, I will help you."

I followed her. She gave me some ointment to rub into the soles of my feet, telling me that it bestowed the siddhi of fleetness of foot. After I rubbed the ointment into my soles, we flew off more quickly than birds. We soon reached a land filled with rainbows and the beautiful fragrance of flowers. All the ground there was springy and made of light. The whole land was filled with bright red light in every direction. When I looked at my own body I saw that it had become as insubstantial as a reflection in a mirror.

The bhikshuni pointed her finger at a massive palace blazing with light and said, "This palace is called Garuda Peak; whatever aspirations you make within its walls will be accomplished."

The entrances to the palace were patrolled by many guards and soaring vultures. On its first floor were all the Buddhas mentioned in the *Sutra of Three Parts*; I could hear their spontaneous speech. I began to realize that I was no longer in the human world.

Looking over thirty-seven rooftops I saw all the sugatas of the eight dispensations, so bright that my eyes couldn't bear looking at them, like sunlight reflected on water.

A woman holding a skull cup wrapped in green silk approached me. From the center of two wheels, one spinning clockwise and the other counterclockwise, both resting on a double platform, she scooped up blood and gave it to me. In a state of extraordinary faith I drank it, thinking, "She must be Vajravarahi herself!"

The bhikshuni said to me, "You are extremely fortunate!"

The dakini then empowered and purified me with

white, yellow, red, and green vases. I asked the bhikshuni, "What is this place? Please tell me!"

She answered, "This is the land of rakshasas. This palace is the Lotus Light Palace. On the top floor lives Guru Padma. The realm east of here has ten trillion cities of rakshasas; the dharma of all-pervasive ati flourishes there. The food there is flowers, grain, and samadhi.

"South of here are a hundred and ten thousand cities of rakshasas; the dharma of Supreme Qualities flourishes there. The food there is nutmeg and other fruit of the wish-fulfilling tree.

"West of here are trillions and trillions of rakshasa cities; the dharma of Hayagriva flourishes there. The food and drink there are the naturally flowing amrita of immortality.

"North of here are a hundred million rakshasa cities; the profound dharma of Vajrakila flourishes there. The flesh and blood of Rudra fall like rain there."

Delighted, I used all the strength in my arms and legs to get a good look at the palace from all four directions; I saw wonders one could look at forever without satiation.

The bhikshuni pointed downward and said, "Down there is Nyangka Valley in Kongpo."

When I looked, it was utterly dark. I asked the bhikshuni, "Will you ask on my behalf if I might be permitted to remain here and not return to Kongpo?"

She replied, "This is just a good dream. One day, however, this entire realm will really be yours!"

I climbed up to the top floor of the palace.

The great master Guru Rinpoche, Padma Öbar, was sitting there.[26] Lustrously brilliant, he was too bright to look at, like the reflection of the sun in a mirror. He held a longevity vase in his two hands, which rested in his lap, and was surrounded by countless vidyadharas wearing pandit hats. I recognized a few of them, but there were many more I did not. They all gazed at me with delight, chanting proclamations of auspiciousness. Musical instruments played themselves.

26. Padma Öbar, Brilliant Lotus, is a peaceful form of Guru Rinpoche and the principal deity in the *Embodiment of the Three Jewels.*

From the sky fruit somewhat like grapes and other feast food fell like snow and remained floating in the air. Everything desirable just appeared in front of us in great spontaneity; there was no kneading of dough or boiling of water for tea.

The entire palace and all within and outside it were transparent and unobstructed, beyond what reason could encompass. Although there were no earth and stones or feeling of heat and cold – really, no sense of solidity at all – there was still a tremendous clarity to my spontaneous mindfulness.

Guru Rinpoche gave me many blessings then, and many instructions. He said, "May the channel-knots of your karmically ripened physical body of relative truth be untied! May your inhalation and exhalation of breath cease! May your white and red elements melt into the bliss of simplicity! May wisdom winds enter your central channel! May the appearance of day and night be transformed into the luminosity of sleep! May you remain in the state of the great perfection, inseparable from Padmavajra in supreme unity!"

My mind stopped for a long time after Guru Rinpoche said that. Then I looked at him and found that what I was looking at and the person looking had mixed inseparably. Directions no longer had any meaning. I remained immersed in the single sphere of the dharmakaya for a long time.

When I arose from that I found myself in a state where Guru Rinpoche's body and his realm were inseparable. I saw countless mandalas of vidyadharas.

Then I descended to the balcony of the middle floor. I saw the Buddha Akshobhya, Baishajyaguru, and the latter's seven brothers, all of them as vivid as if physically present.

The ground floor had nine concentric courtyards. I entered the innermost one and found the glorious Intersex Protector surrounded by all sorts of other protectors. That courtyard was filled with a lake of blood, brains, and fat, and contained a vast and terrifying tent and fence made entirely of various weapons. Among the protectors there, both Rahula and Vajrasadhu smiled warmly at me.

No matter what direction I looked at, everything was filled with light rays, an indivisible unity of vivid lucidity and emptiness.

Then Guru Rinpoche taught me dharma he named *Pointing Out the Trikaya: Buddhahood in the Palm of*

Your Hand, the Quintessence of Wisdom. He empowered me so that I not forget this instruction, and gave me many further transmissions. I felt satisfied.

In a moment I then found myself in a place where all the ground was golden green. A lot of male and female beings were there, praying to Guru Rinpoche. In front of each of them appeared a Guru Rinpoche of the same size as that being, teaching them dharma. This increased my faith even more. I asked the bhikshuni, "What is this place called?"

She replied, "This is the outer, surrounding island of rakshasas. Everyone born here achieves irreversibility. They are people of middling or poor capacity who practiced Guru Rinpoche's terma."

I thought, "Of poor capacity they may be, but when you compare them to dharma practitioners in the human world, all these beings have achieved rainbow light bodies!"

In another moment we came to a place where all the ground was bright pink, with a river that emitted the sound of the Sanskrit vowels and consonants. I asked the bhikshuni, "What is this place?"

She answered, "This place is called Land of Self-Liberated Suffering and Habits. Everyone born here is someone who received empowerment and transmission of Guru Padma's profound terma. Beyond here is a land filled with people of five different races. All born there once tasted samaya substances from Guru Padma's profound terma. In that land even the word *suffering* is unknown. All they do there is train in the virtues of the stages and paths; they are naturally diligent."

I thought of how happy all these people were, especially in comparison to people in the human world.

After another moment we came to a place filled with horses of conch, birds of turquoise, yaks and cattle of copper, fish of gold, frogs of turquoise, other birds of silver, and many other species of animals, all their bodies formed from precious materials. They were all grazing on green grass, fruit, and rivers of milk, and happily playing with one another in fields filled with lovely flowers. It was amazing: none of them were engaged in any wrongdoing. I asked the bhikshuni, "What caused these beings to be born here?"

She replied, "They are the rebirths of animals who were killed so their flesh could be used in feast offerings or special accomplishment assemblies. They have been reborn here, and with the bodies they have, because of the connection formed by their flesh and blood."

After that we reached a place where the land and water appeared solid and ordinary. There was also a gentle breeze. Then we came to a place with a few mountains, some forested and some bare rock, and even some dolomite deposits. On its uplands various crops were growing. I asked the bhikshuni, "What is this land?"

She answered, "This is the outer edge of the rakshasa lands. Those born here are those who formed only a slight connection with Guru Rinpoche's profound terma. They practice dharma here, and eventually reach the central palace, Garuda Peak. From here, if you cross a great river and a great pass you'll reach Tibet."

In another moment we came to a place where there were a lot of dogs; I was frightened of them. An elderly monk appeared, with white hair and shiny robes. He looked like a great monastic elder, and protected me from the dogs, showing me which way to walk. He said, "You are now freed from harm from dogs." He also told me that he was the mahapandit Shakya Shri, the great disciple of Punyakaragupta.

Continuing on our way back to Tibet we came upon a few Asian tantrikas, enjoying a feast circle and drinking tea. They appeared very pleased to see me, so I asked the bhikshuni, "Who are they?"

She replied, "They are tertöns, the nine called Lingpa, the five called Drimey, Nyangral Nyima Özer, Guru Chöwang, and the vidyadhara Vulture Feather."

They prostrated to the bhikshuni and displayed tremendous respect for her, so I asked one of them, "Who is this bhikshuni?"

He laughed and said, "You've spent all this time with her and still don't know who she is? She is Vajrayogini, the mother of all victors of the three times!"

I felt intensely regretful, and said to the bhikshuni, "I apologize and confess before you; I didn't recognize you!"

The bhikshuni answered me in song sweeter than a horn:

HRIH! GURU PADMA SIDDHI HUM HRIH HRIH!
This place we call the Glorious Copper-Colored
Mountain on Chamaradvipa;
Isn't it really your body, appearance and emptiness
inseparable?
Lord Padmasambhava;
Isn't he really your relaxed, unaltered mind?

Your mind that appears as so many things;
Isn't it really the light of the primordially pure
ground?
All these colors we see;
Aren't they really apparitions of our karmic winds?

If you don't know many to be one,
A deer's horns will never defeat a dog.
If your mind doesn't look at itself,
You'll fail no matter what else you know.
If you don't realize the kayas and wisdoms,
All your lectures won't make you a buddha.

The highlands and snowy peaks of mountains,
The lowlands with their forests and springs,
And all the rocky slopes in between;
No matter where you go, you won't find anything
other than your mind.

Don't forget this; keep it all in your mind.
AH! AH! AH!

I said, "I take refuge in you! I didn't know you were the wisdom dakini!" In response she sang again, as sweetly as a lute:

HRIH! True! No one knows themselves.
You are like children scolding their reflection in a mirror.
You've no idea of the treasure within your poor man's hovel.
Bewildered by your own light rays in the bardo
You bind yourselves like silkworms.
Your knots must untie themselves like a coiled snake.

Appearances and mind are inseparable, born together.
Spontaneous lucidity-emptiness, I am the mother of all samsara and nirvana.
Outwardly, I am the dakini of the charnel grounds.
Inwardly, I am the twenty-one Taras.
Secretly, I am the dakinis of the five families.
In suchness I am the dharmakaya, the great mother.

Outwardly, I am the twelve earth goddesses.
Inwardly, I am Vajravarahi.
Secretly, I am Yeshe Tsogyal.
In nondual suchness I am Samantabhadri.

Outwardly, I am the mothers, the five elements.
Inwardly, I am the five offering goddesses.
Secretly, I am Ekajati, the protectress of mantra.
In suchness I am the indivisible expanse of space,
All-pervading, utterly pure, all-creating, yet without
any substance.
I am the channels, winds, essence, and avadhuti.
Never forget me; keep me in mind.

At that moment I began to pass through the stages of emergence from sleep – the reversal of the appearance, increase, and attainment through which one falls asleep. In a state of vivid awareness, I woke up and thought to myself, "Oh, mother! I wish I hadn't woken up from that dream!" I immediately wrote the dream down by the light of a butter lamp.

KTD Publications

Karma Triyana Dharmachakra (KTD) is the North American seat of the Gyalwang Karmapas of the 900-year-old Karma Kagyu lineage of Tibetan Buddhism, which is a guide to millions of Buddhists around the world. The present Karmapa is the 17th Gyalwang Karmapa, Ogyen Trinley Dorje.

KTD Publications, a part of Karma Triyana Dharmachakra, is a not-for-profit publisher established with the purpose of facilitating the projects and activities manifesting from the inspiration and blessings of the 17th Gyalwang Karmapa, Ogyen Trinley Dorje.

We are dedicated to gathering the garlands of precious teachings of the past and present and producing fine-quality books. Our focus is on works that have never before been published, such as Karma Chakme's *Mountain Dharma*, works that have never before been translated, such as *Garland of Jewels* and *The First Karmapa*, original works such as *Siddhas of Ga*, and special edition books such as *Celebrating Karmapa* and *Dharma King*.

www.ktdpublications.com
KTD Publications
335 Meads Mountain Road
Woodstock NY 12498
845.679.5906 extension 1050
845.332.3031 mobile

Environmental Impact Statement

In fulfillment of His Holiness's wish to protect the environment and minimize our eco footprint, as a "green publisher," KTD Publications is concerned about the future of the world's endangered forests and committed to the responsible use of natural resources. When possible, our books include an environmental audit conducted by our printers, quantifying environmental impact and benefit due to printing processes, ink, paper, and transportation choices for a given publication.

green press INITIATIVE

KTD Publications is committed to preserving ancient forests and natural resources. We elected to print this title on 100% post consumer recycled paper, processed chlorine free. As a result, for this printing, we have saved:

8 Trees (40' tall and 6-8" diameter)
3,624 Gallons of Wastewater
7 Million BTUs of Total Energy
365 Pounds of Solid Waste
1,100 Pounds of Greenhouse Gases

KTD Publications made this paper choice because our printer, Thomson-Shore, Inc., is a member of Green Press Initiative, a nonprofit program dedicated to supporting authors, publishers, and suppliers in their efforts to reduce their use of fiber obtained from endangered forests.

For more information, visit www.greenpressinitiative.org

Environmental impact estimates were made using the Environmental Defense Paper Calculator. For more information visit: www.papercalculator.org.

May All Beings Be Happy